This book is dedicated to the millions of Lesbians and Gay men
who do not tell the church who they are because they know that the
church prefers not to hear the truth.

LOVING WOMEN

/ LOVING MEN

GAY LIBERATION
AND THE CHURCH

Edited / Authored by
Sally Gearhart and William R. Johnson

PUBLICATIONS

Library of Congress Cataloging in Publication Data
Gearhart, Sally Miller, 1931-
  Loving women/loving men.
  1. Homosexuality and Christianity. 2. Gay
liberation movement. I. Johnson, William Reagan,
1946-   joint author. II. Title.
BR115.H6G4   261.8'34'157   74-11339
ISBN 0-912078-41-3

Production by: David Charlsen
               Douglas Mount And Others
Designed by: Zoe Brown

CONTENTS

INTRODUCTION

For several years both of us have been speaking out in our separate ways about ourselves and about the health and joy of same-sex relationships. We have spoken in schools and seminaries, to police, psychiatrists, medical doctors, social workers, lawyers, government officials, businesswomen and businessmen. We've talked with parents, teenagers, senior citizens, people of all political persuasions and people of all sexual preferences.

Whenever we address the conflict between society's attitudes and the lives of Gay people, we always seem to come back to the church, back to the directives of the Old Testament and to what both Law and Gospel have become in 1974. Our legal system, which would classify us and all other Gay people as criminals, is based on British common law. This in turn originated in Judeo-Christian doctrine. The medical and psychiatric professionals who label us "deviant" ultimately admit that their view of homosexuality as a "sickness" is heavily influenced by two or three thousand years' worth of Judeo-Christian tradition. That tradition is woven into the fabric of every analyst's personal history and environment. And the same is true for every citizen of the Western world.

It is true that on December 15, 1973 the trustees of the American Psychiatric Association adopted a resolution, later affirmed by a referendum vote of the APA membership, officially to remove homosexuality from its catalogue of mental disorders and to urge that homosexuals be given all the protection from discrimination now guaranteed to other citizens. The APA action was the result of a ten-year confrontation and lobbying effort by Gay activists. Though highly significant, this action is only a small step in the long and continuing struggle, for the old scriptural influences will not be eradicated overnight.

In addition, the attitude of educators, members of the "helping" professions, law-enforcement agents and business people is grounded in the precepts of Judeo-Christian morality. What is considered "sick" or "illegal" or "immature" in our culture is deemed so because those precepts have subtly become a part of our thinking in Western culture. Even the atheist does not escape this influence.

Clearly, then, the church must be approached directly about the injustices Gay people suffer at its hands. Even more clearly, it cannot be approached by Gay people who are "in the closet." (Gay persons are said to be "in the closet" when, for the sake of their economic and psychological survival, they pretend that they are what society assumes them to be: heterosexuals.) Direct action must be taken by Gay people who have some care for and/or investment in the church and in the tradition that has to one degree or another molded us all.

Both of us are openly Gay people whose relationship with the church is direct and whose concern for its people is deep. Bill is ordained in the United Church of Christ and is presently Executive Director of the Council on Religion and the Homosexual. He is a member of the National Task Force on Gay People in the Church. Sally received her Ph.D. in 1956 from the University of Illinois and has spent most of her professional life within the Methodist and Lutheran traditions, teaching in church-affiliated colleges. We have joined here in an effort to present information and to advocate beliefs and actions that the church does not wish to consider. The factual data, presented for the most part in Chapters 1, 2, 3, and the Bibliography, reflects the experience of people intimately involved with the church—laypeople and clergy, women and men, Gay people and heterosexuals. In Chapters 4 and 5 we speak as Gay people and present our advocacy.

The writing in Chapters 4 and 5 and to some degree in Chapter 3 is extremely critical of the church. From our perspective as Gay people the institutional church must be understood to be an oppressor. We know of the pain that Lesbians and Gay men suffer within the church; we understand something of the fear and ignorance that dehumanize them there. With this book we hope to speak to these Gay sisters and brothers and we hope to reach with lasting effect those who oppress them.

We urge the reader to think of this book as a beginning, as a voice calling to the church in order to initiate dialogue. The issues raised here are important, but they only begin to challenge the misconceptions and prejudices that have held Gay people down for so long.

We do not presume to represent or to speak for all Gay people. We are Gay. We can say that aloud and without fear. We can speak out partly because of our immediate environment and circumstances, partly because of our individual identities, and partly because of good fortune. We are two among millions. Much of what we say will resonate with Gay people. Some may not. We hope we will be understood as two people who are a part of a larger community of persons who would speak their truths to the church if they felt free to do so and if they sensed that they would be heard.

Though there is nothing to guarantee that a Gay-male-Gemini minister born with the nuclear age could work with a Lesbian-feminist-Aries teacher who remembers the fireside chats of FDR, the combination has worked out fine. We have drunk a lot of coffee and talked about a lot of things. We have criticized each other promptly, renewed one another's spirits, and spoken in tongues with Bill's dog Rye when diversion was essential to our mental health. We have a great deal of respect for each other above and beyond our disagreements—disagreements which, surprisingly enough, are more in the realm of theology than on female/male issues.

Our thanks go to many people outside and inside the church, clergy and laity, Gay and not Gay. Some who have touched this book most deeply are Rachel Barnsley, Peggy Cleveland, Louis Crompton, Jean Crosby, L. William Eichhorn, Ruth Gottstein, Susan Halverstadt, Dale Hempen, William Kruse, John Rogers, Pat Smith, Michael Steeb and Peggy Way. We are especially grateful for the long and constant inspiration of Del Martin and Phyllis Lyon.

Sally Gearhart
Bill Johnson

July 1974
San Francisco

During our work together
I have grown confident in and been supported by
Bill's growing feminist consciousness. The political
decision to commit myself to publishing through an
establishment press was not an easy one. To agree to go
that route accompanied by a Gay man gave me still
more difficulty; initially such a proposal
did not sit well with my staunch separatist feelings—
for I had long believed that at this point in history it
was impossible for women and men to work together
constructively. Fortunately, the staff of
Glide Publications is more human and life-loving
than any we have met or heard of; they helped to allay
a lot (but not all) of my fears about publishing.
And working with Bill has gone a long way in
convincing me that "careful coalitions" are possible when
each party respects the ground
on which the other stands. In him I have discovered
a strong, gentle person and I have done some real
growing because of him. It has been a rich experience.

Sally Gearhart

I was apprehensive about Sally in the
beginning, mostly because her feminism precedes
her by about a quarter of a mile,
but I was eager to learn from her. During
our first conversation my apprehension began to turn
into expectation and enjoyment. We
talked very frankly about whether or not we
could work together and actually produce the kind
of book we envisioned. We discussed
the tender spots in each of our egos; we
considered how broke we were and wondered
whether or not it was opportunistic
to write about being Gay; we talked seriously about how
we should handle any money that might come
to us from the book. We found
that we have a common concern for
Gay people and for church people and
we agreed that as many people as possible should
have a chance to read the material by
Donald Kuhn and Robert Treese and to hear what
Gay people have to say about
ourselves and about the church. My respect for Sally
as a prophetic and loving woman has grown.
She has touched my life deeply and enabled me to
see myself more honestly. It has been a rich experience.

Bill Johnson

*Donald Kuhn is a minister of
Temple United Methodist Church in San Francisco.
He was formerly Director of Communications
at Glide Urban Center, also in San Francisco.
This article
is an account of a consultation which resulted in the
founding of the Council on Religion and the Homosexual
in May, 1964. It has been considerably but not essentially
altered and abbreviated. We hope we have maintained
the flow and spirit of the consultation
without reporting the details of every presentation.
In order to
preserve the flavor of the mid-1960's we have left
unchanged the heavily sexist language of the article
and that of the persons quoted in it. The uses of the
generic masculine—"he," "his," "him," "man," and
"mankind" to include all people, the unfailing primary
position of "men" when both "men and women" are
mentioned, continued reference to the church as female,
and the assumption of God's masculine gender—all
reflect the general level of consciousness, even of people
trying their best to abolish prejudice. Except where
otherwise indicated, the term "homosexual" probably
refers to a man. "Gay," though it had not the militancy
that it has in 1974, did have meaning ten years ago
beyond its own subculture; however, it was still often
uttered with vocal quotation marks. The words
"homophile" and "homosexual," used almost exclusively
throughout this article, are regarded by most Gay people
today as either dated, clinical or unliberated. The use of
such terms highlights the changes that a decade has made.
Sexist or
heterosexist language notwithstanding, this article records
a milestone in the history of the Gay movement. To
look back on where we've been and to discover "early
courage" among both Gay people and church people
is both sobering and strengthening.—Eds.*

THE CHURCH AND THE HOMO-SEXUAL

DONALD KUHN

HOW IT STARTED

"Forget who you represent. We represent the human race. Let's start there."
This is how Ted McIlvenna began his presentation to the thirty informally
dressed men and women who sat around a fire at the United Church of Christ's

This material has been excerpted from *The Church and the Homosexual: A Report on a
Consultation*, prepared by Donald Kuhn and published in pamphlet form by Glide Publications. The pamphlet is available from the Council on Religion and the Homosexual,
83 McAllister Street, Suite 421, San Francisco, California 94102 at $1.00 per copy.

3

White Memorial Retreat in Mill Valley outside San Francisco. It was 10:00 p.m.
on Sunday, May 31, 1964, but the consultation had been a long time in the
making. The man standing before the group, Ted McIlvenna, had started it all.
As director of the Young Adult Project in San Francisco Ted had met persons
for whom homosexuality in some way created problems. He began looking
for groups which provided services for homosexuals, and he found four: the
Daughters of Bilitis, the Mattachine Society, Inc., the League for Civil Education and the Tavern Guild. During his search, Ted learned how sharp the
division was between homosexuals and the church*—at least in the minds of
many homosexuals.

Ted told Charles Mowry of Methodism's Older Youth / Young Adult Project what he had learned. Charles in turn conferred with Roger Burgess and
Dale White of the Division of Alcohol Problems and General Welfare of the
Methodist Board of Christian Social Concerns. These two agencies decided to
join the Glide Urban Center in sponsoring a consultation which would include
representatives from homophile organizations and churches. Glide's Lewis
Durham and Ted McIlvenna were asked to prepare for a San Francisco consultation and to extend invitations. They did so, working closely with the
four homosexual groups in developing plans for the meeting.

BEFORE THE CONSULTATION

A good deal of preparation for the consultation's regular sessions was necessary, for even the vocabulary of the homosexual world was strange to churchmen. It was decided that, as an introductory activity, groups of delegates
would visit bars that catered to male homosexuals. On the Saturday evening
before the consultation, then, participants met at the Precarious Vision, a
church-sponsored coffee house on Bush Street in San Francisco, and from
there members of the Mattachine Society accompanied them on a tour of the
city's wide variety of homosexual gathering places—not only bars but coffee
houses where the clientele could include teenagers as well as older men. Delegates saw gay men in all manner of dress from tee shirts and "drag" to
"leather" and conservative business suits; they experienced firsthand the week-

*We have left up to the individual contributor the choice of whether to capitalize such
terms as "Bible," "Church," "God," "Scriptures," "Gay," and "Lesbian." We felt that
this allowed each writer her/his own freedom and preserved the integrity of each individual contribution.—Eds.

end life of the most visible part of the homophile population. The footsore churchmen, as unaccustomed to late Saturday nights as to the gay bar circuit, returned to their hotel rooms in the early hours of the morning.

Near noon on Sunday, still bleary-eyed from the night before, they gathered to eat lunch and then depart for a picnic sponsored by the League for Civil Education. Homosexual members of the consultation—seemingly an unsleeping population— had left earlier for the picnic, there to enjoy the unlimited food, beer and soft drinks. The participants travelled for several hours, finally passing through a bumpy pasture to a secret oceanside location. There they discovered about a hundred men and women from the homophile community. Some sat on the ground talking and eating; others were involved in sports activities; still others were holding each other or exchanging gestures of affection. The food at the picnic, the company, and the remoteness of the location seemed to conspire against a prompt beginning of the opening session. From the picnic grounds the participants drove to the retreat center where the consultation officially and belatedly began.

THE OPENING SESSION

After most of the delegates had arrived, Lewis Durham, the coordinator of the event, led the group in some traditional "getting-acquainted" rituals. Then Ted McIlvenna, the only person in the group who was known to everyone there, laid the groundwork for subsequent discussion. He cautioned against "letting sexual identification get in the way of intelligent understanding." Neither the heterosexuals nor the homosexuals were acknowledged to have special access to truth or righteousness. Even deference to women was dropped—at their request. "Being nice to avoid disagreement" was discouraged and it was agreed that "mutual understanding" was to be the goal of the sessions. Preachers were cautioned against looting for sermons and nonpreachers were urged not to write off ministers as having nothing relevant to offer.

After the opening statements, the participants headed for the coffee pot, many of them admitting bewilderment and frustration. They knew some practical things—like where to find towels and when meals were to be served—but as to the business at hand, even vocabulary, it seemed, was going to be a struggle: how to use words with only a single meaning? A host of unanswered questions seemed to confront the entire group. One churchman said to another over his coffee, "It's all too personal, too limited, too ill-defined."

MONDAY MORNING

The next morning the group began its first work session. According to the program the topic of the day was "How we view each other—and how we hope the relationships might be."

C. Kilmer (Kim) Myers of Chicago's Urban Training Center spoke first about how churchmen view homosexuals. He pointed out that the church's attitude is not one that can be readily identified since most denominational bodies do not have "official statements" on either homosexuals or homosexuality. Yet the church, like other groups, has been conditioned, Kim said, by prevailing sexual patterns, especially by sexual taboos. Accordingly, churchmen as individuals are often silent on the subject and if pressed, their attitudes vary from utter rejection to complete acceptance; often fear and hostility are the basis for these attitudes.

Kim observed that though over time a consistency in sexual patterns is common—that is, heterosexuality has been taken to be the norm—still the church is beginning to recognize a new pluralism in this area. It is again identifying itself with God's People regardless of how society identifies a group or how that group identifies itself. He cautioned participants against dwelling in the past and encouraged the group to project new paths appropriate for a new age.

THE MALE COMMUNITY SPEAKS

Mattachine's Don Lucas, speaking on behalf of male homosexuals, shared with the group some impressive testimonial evidence that he had gathered especially for the consultation. He had invited 150 men believed to be homosexuals to answer anonymously specific questions about the church, its attitude toward and its relationship to homosexuals and homosexuality. The forty respondents were from thirteen states and ranged in age from sixteen to forty-four; they were Roman Catholic, Protestant, and atheist. Among them were college professors, a Methodist minister, a public-relations director of a Protestant denomination, a Presbyterian director of youth work and music, a military man and a business management advisor.

For some of the respondents "the church" connoted the organized entity while for others it meant the people who make up the church. The consensus was that the church is clearly letting the homosexual down, at least in the communities from which the responses came. It chooses to ignore the subject of homosexuality and therefore fails to acknowledge a significant portion of its consituency. Actually, Don said, the church's attitude toward such issues as birth control and divorce reveal it to be not so much anti-homosexual as anti-sexual. For instance, according to respondents, the church needs to recognize the fact that sex has meaning and value outside the function of procreation. All in all, respondents found church doctrine to be far behind twentieth-century knowledge and experience. Some felt that a change in doctrine would help the homosexual; one recommended that homosexual marriage be performed in and sanctioned by the church. Still others felt that any change would only be a compromise—that fundamentally churchmen would still want to see the change come about in the homosexual and not in the church. This attitude seemed to be most common to Roman Catholics.

There were three distinct attitudes expressed in regard to joining a church: one group of respondents would definitely join if the church changed its attitudes toward homosexuality; a second group did not know, but doubted that they would even if those attitudes changed; a final group would not join under any circumstances. Of the forty individuals, fourteen—or thirty-five percent—belonged to and were active in a church, four persons held memberships but did not attend, and over half the group—twenty-two people—did not associate with the church at all. Those who did belong indicated that they remained out of a desire for the comfort and spiritual nourishment that the church could offer; but they believed that they would be totally rejected were the church to learn about their homosexuality.

Most of the respondents were raised in a church setting and most felt that their early church training had not only brought them to Christ Awareness but had given them as well an intellectually stimulating beginning to life. At about the age of puberty, however, the respondents found that the church was not dealing with the thousands of questions they had regarding sexuality and their own sexual drives. The church, they concluded, refused to understand the phenomenon of homosexuality. One man stated, "The church does not understand the homosexual and does not understand a large percent of human beings." Another suggested that the church does not understand because it is afraid to delve into the subject.

When Don invited the forty respondents to suggest changes, they offered a variety of ideas, among them that the church should leave sexual matters to individual conscience, that it should accept people as people, that it should redefine the concept of "sin" and study in depth the subject of homosexuality; in short, they felt the church should update its thinking in all areas. Particularly, the suggestions went on, the clergy should be educated about sexuality and that subject should be made a part of the church's education program for children and young people. One respondent called for the National Council of Churches to make an affirmative statement about homosexuality.

Don then read the letter of a sixteen-year-old Roman Catholic respondent. The tone of the letter alternated between puzzlement and scepticism on the one hand and fear and pain of condemnation on the other:

> How am I supposed to know what my Creator thinks
> of me? The church says that God thinks I am a
> "monster" but throughout my whole life I've received
> the sacraments, done good and bad things, sinned and
> confessed. Now since a couple of months ago I am
> "against nature" and if I don't change I'm doomed . . . .
> Even though my mind thinks that love is more important
> than just heterosexual or homosexual love, my soul
> and heart can never be at peace . . . .
>   If I tell you that I was under good influence, then
> I'm not doing justice to myself and to my situation.
> If I tell you that I was under bad influence, I'm not
> doing justice to God, which is automatically a sin.
> What a predicament! . . . I can't bring myself to believe
> I am "abnormal" or a "criminal against society" . . . .
> How is the church going to know how I feel? A person
> or a group should experience the feeling of being a
> "monster" or "abnormal degenerate" before judging
> it . . . . If the church came to its senses and stopped
> condemning then so would the majority of society . . . .
> Please don't make me feel I'll go straight to Hell—
> at least send me to Purgatory so I'll have a chance
> to progress.

Don closed his presentation with his own analysis. He pinpointed the homosexual's "problem" as a feeling that he is rejected and misunderstood. The

THE CHURCH AND THE HOMOSEXUAL

homosexual feels that the church more than any other institution in society should accept and understand him; yet the church holds up a mirror that reflects only an image of perversion. The homosexual feels the church to be wrong, but his heritage tells him that it is the infallible word of God which is condemning him—and in that conflict lies the seed of neurosis. It is incumbent upon the church, Don continued, to prepare to deal compassionately and knowledgeably with all who seek understanding, particularly the homosexual:

> *The homosexual is a human being. He has a soul and*
> *Christ Consciousness just as do all other human beings.*
> *He loves, lives, and has feelings and emotions which are*
> *really no different from those of his so-called hetero-*
> *sexual counterpart. All human beings are looking for*
> *understanding, love, and approval. The homosexual is*
> *no exception. The church is best suited to demonstrate*
> *to all human beings these qualities, because they are of*
> *a primarily spiritual nature.*

THE WOMEN SPEAK

Billie Talmij of the Daughters of Bilitis spoke on "how we view each other." "The orthodox God of orthodox religion," she began, "is a flat, unmitigated failure. George Bernard Shaw said that. He also said that man had created God in man's own image and then deliberately broken the mold into a thousand small, hard, inflexible pieces and scattered it. Each fragment was quickly caught up—still small, still hard, still inflexible—to become the tenets and dogmas of a thousand Protestant divisions." Billie was inclined to agree with Shaw. But, she said, we homosexuals are more than a little defensive.

> *And who can blame us? We have been called*
> *"unnatural" for eons. Even though there is nothing*
> *alien or unnatural about the act of homosexuality in*
> *Mother Nature herself, the thief feels that he is better*
> *than the homosexual. The man who rapes his child,*
> *physically and mentally, feels he is above the homo-*
> *sexual. The liar slanders him. The adulterer despises him.*
> *Yet can the experts tell us which one of the Ten*

> Commandments the homosexual, just by being
> homosexual, has broken? So the homosexual may be
> more than a little defensive. We are also more than a
> little prejudiced.

Billie explained that in the Daughters of Bilitis there is an activity called
"The Gab'n Java" which is an informal type of discussion.

> Since the four of us who represent the lesbian
> counterpart of this distinguished team were to the last
> one of us non-churchgoers, we felt a little inadequate
> to speak on the church aspect of this situation. So we
> took the topic to one of our Gab'n Javas and found
> some interesting statistics.
>
> Of the twenty-five women present, only two still
> went to church regularly. Of the remaining twenty-
> three, only another two actually quit going to church
> because of their homosexuality. The other two women
> stopped attending long before they were consciously
> aware of their homosexuality. We also found that,
> because we did not attend church we were outdated
> in our notions about church and clergymen. I for one
> found that my strongest image of a churchman was
> the hard-shelled Baptist preacher who shouted hell, fire,
> and damnation from the pulpit, who refused to utter
> the dirty word, sex, and who later tore the blouse from
> a fourteen-year-old girl whom he tried to seduce in the
> choir loft.
>
> So when I say we are more than a little prejudiced,
> I am including each of us, for there is not a person in
> this room who doesn't have preconceived notions about
> this subject of the church and homosexuality—regardless
> of his or her sexual proclivities, sexual activities, or
> sexual anxieties.
>
> If there is such a thing as original sin, then to me it
> is the sin of ignorant, inflexible, wall-to-wall thinking.
> I would venture to say that each of us in this respect

is an original sinner. So we of the Daughters of Bilitis offer
a challenge to "gay" and "straight" alike, a challenge to
shake the bricks in this four-walled thinking. We offer
you some demolition fuses, some ideas to contemplate,
to renovate. Some of these ideas are bombs that may
blow up tempers. Some may fizzle and not last the week.
Some are slow-burning "sleepers" guaranteed maybe
much later to dislodge a brick or two on both sides of
the wall.

Billie then presented about seventy of the "demolition fuses," short rapid-fire, concisely worded ideas. Often they were quotations from authoritative sources; sometimes they were epigrammatic; all of them were concerned with religion, sexuality and human relations. They called homosexuals as well as "straight" people to a reassessment of themselves.

The fuses suggested, for instance, that the church hears Law before it hears love, that it is deaf to Jesus' words "judge not;" that having lost sight of its purpose the church has become authoritative and corrupt; that because of its rigidity it is losing not only members but influence. Billie's "fuses" also suggested that homosexuals are scapegoats for society's guilt; that homosexuals often identify themselves too much with the label "homosexual" and not enough with the label "human;" that above all young people who are identifying as homosexuals need counselling and understanding; that the "neurosis" suffered by many homosexual people has its roots in rigid church training. About love, sexuality and living, Billie suggested that to fulfill the self is to fulfill God; that sexuality, so varied in its expression, is God-given and to deny it is to betray a gift of God; that all are sinners and that determining "greater" or "lesser" sins is difficult; that as far as influence on the young is concerned it is not homosexuality that is destructive but attitudes in this country toward all of human sexuality.

Billie concluded by saying that most homosexuals have to face some kind of contradiction between their lives and the doctrines of the church; few, she said, can live with such a schism, in two such conflicting worlds. Thus more often than not it is the church that is rejected—not God, but the institution which has misunderstood God's purpose.

Billie's presentation ended the formal exchange of "how we view each other."

A question and answer session followed and then the participants divided into three groups for discussion. The groups, stirred as well as informed by the words of the speakers, seemed to jump from one topic to another, asking questions and rarely touching upon concrete answers. Who is the scapegoat— the homosexual or the church? Is the homosexual or the heterosexual normal? What causes homosexuality? Is sex, masculinity, femininity natural? What characteristic distinguishes a person as a homosexual? What are the criteria by which a combination of people may be considered a family?

Every person contributed to the small-group discussions, responding rapidly and candidly. Each person answered questions without hesitation. While there was seldom pause in the conversation, still the small groups could be called listening groups. No one tried to sell a cause or to defend a party line. The groups continued their sharing well into the "free time."

THE RIGHT TO HIDE

"Queers and niggers are responsible for all crime and venereal disease." These were the opening words of Guy Strait's informal presentation on behalf of the League for Civil Education. He continued, "Both are lazy, unstable, and incapable of responsible participation in society. Unfortunately these stereotypes apparently dominate the thinking of lawmakers and law enforcement personnel. But the homosexual has an advantage over the Negro. He can hide."

Guy then gave an account of California's sex laws and made painfully clear the manner in which these laws are enforced—that is, almost exclusively against homosexual men. The law against wandering, for instance, allows police to arrest a person for windowshopping. (If he has the time and $500, a man can beat the charge in court.) For oral copulation the sentence is five years to life; for masturbation from six to fifteen years. "If everyone who violated one of California's sex laws were arrested," Guy said, "there would be no one left to guard the jails."

He pointed out the absurdity of such sex laws: a man with a case of dysentery remaining in the rest room too long could be picked up on a sex charge; a man putting his hand on the arm of another man is subject to arrest; even politicians kissing babies could be prosecuted under child molesting laws. The purpose of such laws, Guy said, was to prevent events which might follow.

Yet the laws constitute legislation against a class of people, against homosexuals, for they are selectively enforced; if you're not a homosexual, your breaking the law will probably be ignored.

Guy touched upon the consequences of such arrests. Whether or not the person is found guilty, jobs and whole careers are ruined. It is impossible for a person to secure or retain a teaching certificate, for instance, after one such arrest. He then pointed to the clergy as responsible for the maintenance of the sex laws and their selective enforcement:

> These laws have remained unchanged because of the clergy. The legislature is afraid of the clergy. Both clergymen and legislators are afraid to speak out for homosexuals because someone may think that they are homosexuals—the sure-fire end of a ministry or a political career. With the knowledge that if they tackle the sex laws they will be crucified, politicians identify with the church against the homosexual.

Guy called for specific reforms:

> A clear delineation of what a sex crime is in the light of the scientific knowledge presently ignored by both church and state.
>
> An erasing from public records—FBI and local—of any arrest not leading to a guilty verdict. "Sex offense" —the term used—is enough in itself to ruin a man's career even if after the charge he was found innocent.
>
> Lifting of the bail for all the miscellaneous acts labelled "sex offense"; there is no need for bail except in the case of a crime-of-violence charge.
>
> Legalization or decriminalization of homosexual relationships between consenting adults.
>
> Granting of equal protection under the law to homosexual people.

Guy's presentation was food for more lively discussion in the small groups. Again, participants talked together far into their unscheduled time. After late afternoon relaxation and dinner they were ready to listen to the Monday evening presentation by Kim Myers.

BIBLICAL AND THEOLOGICAL BASES

Kim opened his remarks, "The Biblical and Theological Bases for Relationship between the Church and the Homosexual," by stating that his whole approach to the question of homosexuality had been mainly a pastoral one. "When a minister enters a pastoral situation, particularly if it's rough, he has no guide, no blueprint except a general grasp of the direction he believes he should go. It is that general direction that I would like to discuss—believing that what I say is biblical and has theological justification."

He noted first that there could be no relationship between church and homosexual unless the church could reassess her view of all of sexuality in the light of modern discoveries, particularly in psychology and sociology. He characterized the church as constantly changing in response to the continuing revelation of truth. Then, Kim said, we need to examine the changes within the church to ascertain whether or not our image of her is an accurate one.

Kim affirmed any relationship as valid if it is informed by love, commitment and responsibility. He spoke of the "justice" that must also inform all love and give it reality beyond mere talk. "We can say, for example, that we love the Negro—and this is being said from white pulpits all over the country. But unless there is a conviction that love finds its concrete expression in justice, then this love is sentimental; it is flat; it is uninformed by justice." He made an appeal for the understanding of Christian symbols—of the virgin birth not as anti-sexual but as exaltation of the principle of femininity in the divine; of St. Paul's "body of this death" not as an image of the body as prisonhouse but as a view of the breakdown of relationships between human beings.

All of us are victims of *angst*, of despair. "When a man reaches out for the other and discovers that somehow he cannot reach the other," the structure of a relationship tumbles down and we are alone. "One might say that if a man has not experienced *angst* he has not experienced separation and perhaps does not understand what reunion is."

Kim recommended an understanding of "grace" as "acceptance." He described moments in which we each feel accepted and suggested we use these moments as a way of understanding St. Paul's doctrine of justification by faith. When for a moment we understand and hear another's anguish, we are re-created, re-formed, and healed. We bridge for a moment the separation of ourselves from the other; we accept and are reconciled.

This acceptance must come through a community of people and a community of memory which is called the church:

> *The church is formed by the memory of the past. The*
> *church views the present moments as the fulfillment and*
> *the consummation of the past and the present. This we*
> *call, in another theological word, eschaton, which is to*
> *say pertaining to the act. Now, therefore, the quality*
> *of life in the community has the eschatological character,*
> *has this character of memory, has the character of the*
> *church always in the process of becoming what she is.*
> *But she never becomes what she is until the eschaton.*
> *This would be said to be the hurdle of the Christian*
> *view of history: the memory of the past, the moment*
> *of the past, the moment, and the future. In a real sense*
> *this is the history of man, the history of each man. So*
> *that this justification comes in the community of*
> *memory, the community of the moment, the com-*
> *munity of the future and is kept alive in the church*
> *through the power of the symbols and the images of*
> *the church which I think may well be universal sym-*
> *bols. When they become less than universal they are*
> *parochial, denominational, narrow, restrictive. When the*
> *symbols are used in a narrow sense the church itself*
> *becomes less than the sacrament of humanity. Then the*
> *church becomes parochial, denominational, bigoted,*
> *"of the day," acculturated.*

"Justification," then, is a moment of acceptance, of accepting the fact that one is accepted. It is a reaching out to and a forming of a union with the other. It could happen, Kim reminded the participants, in a gay bar. It is a moment that can take place in "the entire fabric of life."

Finally, Kim proposed that the New Being—Jesus in Tillich's thought—involves "the new humanity." He explored a host of Christian symbols, showing how the new humanity is expressed in those symbols. Particularly significant is the church as the mother of God, the completion of the symbolism "in which masculinity and femininity are in perfect union and in which the wholeness of man—in his femininity, in his homosexuality, in his heterosexuality—somehow emerges."

Kim concluded by talking of how symbols work on us.

> *They do work on us, all the time, on every one of us. The holy symbols, the symbols which point to the ultimate meaning of life and to our vital concerns have power over us. This is true not when we make moral efforts, not by being better, not by being "gooder," not by adopting the tenets of whatever the morals of the culture might be, not by striving and pushing to keep away from sins. No. It is not this. Yet simply by saying "yes" to the symbol and allowing its power to permeate us, we may learn to accept the fact that we are accepted, that we are at home in the world, and that we belong to the new humanity.*

After this presentation, the group sought symbols which would express the vitality of the Christian religion and fit the experiences of homosexuals. A note of urgency pervaded the discussion. Then, after late-evening coffee, small groups of delegates clustered here and there. But they no longer talked of sex. Everyone seemed to forget his "sex identification." One small group talked politics. Another discussed hunting and church choirs. A bridge game started in another corner. Others, stimulated by Kim's presentation, dug deeper into the meaning of art forms and symbolism. More than being "all sexed out," each person had gotten past the labels—"heterosexual," "homosexual," "churchman"—and had begun to make friends.

THE LAST DAY

According to pre-consultation plans, the final day had been set aside to explore "what kind of statement could be made about the relationship between the church and the homosexual." To prepare the small groups for the task, Ted McIlvenna commented about some of the topics which such a statement might include:

We could include a statement about man—who he is and who we are . . . . Both churchmen and homosexuals use people. This is an admission which needs to be made . . . . In listing sins, we need to include the church's penchant for separating "the good" from "the bad" in a way that neither the experience of history nor the data of the behavioral sciences supports . . . .

We need to remind each other that one status identification does not blot our common humanity. Labeling a person a "homosexual" or a "churchman" does not cancel the humanity of either. The ranks of both the church and the homophile community include some who are "immature," even "infantile," perhaps even "maniacs." But they are not all that way, and none are without God . . . .

Someday soon the church needs to speak from its traditional position as "keeper of morality" and "authority on existence" about whether homosexual acts are "natural" or "unnatural." How do they differ from heterosexual acts? What is the nature of marriage? What sex identification is required by God? How is integrity in intimate relationships to be defined and appraised?

The church needs to acknowledge every man's need for intimacy and if there is a choice between intimacy in the sex act alone or no intimacy at all, the sex act alone needs to be recognized as a moment of eternal encounter. The church needs to remind herself, to tell homosexuals, and to acknowledge to all mankind that being or not being a homosexual is not salvifically important.

We may not be ready to make a definitive statement, but we must at least commit ourselves to continued discussions.

After Ted's remarks, the small groups convened for their final meeting. When the groups made their reports, no one recommended an "official statement." Each group's report was accepted for what it was—the consensus of one group.

Group One's report was in the form of "directions we must take." It condemned the term "crime against nature," and said, "We must accept homosexuality—not encourage it or endorse it. We must remove homosexual behavior among consenting adults from the realm of the law; we must acknowledge that homosexuality per se is neither 'good' nor 'bad.' We must keep the doors of conversation open and swinging both ways."

Group Two described what happened in their group. "We explored how far we could go with each other ideologically; we disseminated facts and each person tried to get into the perspective of each of the others; we dealt with each other gingerly—with sensitivity and acceptance. There was an atmosphere of basic trust and respect. Each 'ministered' to the other. We were 'a religious gay bar.' Finally, we emerged with no panaceas."

Group Three reported that its hours together were times of mutual understanding. While the discussions included a wide variety of topics, a few statements of consensus became possible: "Man has an infinite capacity to love; both society—including homosexual communities—and the churches have sold this capacity short. All people—churchmen and homosexuals—stand under judgment of a moral demand which is a part of man and his societies . . . . Each relationship must be evaluated by the participants according to all that it does to and for the persons involved . . . . Clandestine love carries with it a dark shadow; yet such love may be the highest moral expression possible in specific situations. . . . Calling homosexuality a disease helps no one."

All groups agreed that they had found a meeting ground in their common search for meaning; they requested continuing conversation; and they agreed upon the need for a system of helping troubled teenagers. After farewells, each participant departed knowing that this unique community had spent its moment in history; each knew that the mark of that community's existence could not be erased.

THE COUNCIL ON RELIGION AND THE HOMOSEXUAL

A few days after the consultation, the participants from San Francisco established themselves as the Council on Religion and the Homosexual. The following statement was adopted:

*In order to promote a continuing dialogue between the
church and the homosexual, understand more fully human
sexuality, and promote understanding of the broad variations and manifestations within the spectrum of human
sexuality, the Council on Religion and the Homosexual sets
forth these goals and purposes:*

1. *To orient the clergy on aspects of homosexuality
   (i.e., physical, economic, legal, intellectual, emotional, etc.) in accordance with homosexual
   testimony and available scientific data.*

2. *To encourage pastoral clergy to provide homosexuals
   of both sexes an opportunity to present their
   views on sex, religion, morals, and ethics to lay
   organizations within their churches.*

3. *To open up channels of communication so that
   clergy and lay churchmen may engage in dialogue
   with the homosexual, so that new understandings
   of the church and of religious faith may be
   developed.*

4. *To conscript the aid of religious publications and
   other appropriate communication media urging a
   broadened editorial policy that will include accurate and objective articles on homosexuality.*

5. *To provide an effective voice throughout the nation
   in matters of laws, policies, and penal reforms
   governing adult sexual behavior.*

6. *To encourage the formation of similar councils on
   religion and the homosexual in other areas.*

7. *To help the clergyman better to understand his
   role as counselor in dealing with problems of
   human sexuality in our society, with special
   reference to young people.*

Since the establishment of the Council in early summer of 1964, it has
developed its constitution and by-laws, elected officers yearly, incorporated
under the laws of the state of California, and received tax-exempt status as a
non-profit organization. Its membership is open to any person who identifies

with the purposes of the organization. The monthly meetings of the Board of Directors are open to the public. From 1964 until January 1973, when the Reverend William R. Johnson was called to be Executive Director, Phyllis Lyon coordinated the activities of the Council.

CRH offers an extensive publications service, maintains a speakers' bureau that responds to more than three hundred requests every year, and provides crisis intervention and referral services. Up-to-date information concerning organizing efforts in denominations and seminary communities is on file in the CRH office. The Council's annual symposium on "The Life Styles of the Homosexual" is regarded as the finest of its kind in the country. CRH personnel are available for symposia in locales other than San Francisco. The Council has confronted and initiated dialogue with the police, denominational leaders, and public officials in the city, county, and state government. As such dialogue intensifies, particularly between the church and the homosexual, the leadership of the Council on Religion and the Homosexual will be in evidence.

THE PARTICIPANTS

A committee of leaders in homosexual organizations and staff members from Glide Urban Center and Young Adult Project (in behalf of church sponsors) extended invitations to an equal number of people from churches and homophile organizations. Ultimately, the participants came from Chicago, Minneapolis, Nashville, New York, San Francisco and Washington, D.C. They represented the Daughters of Bilitis, Glide Urban Center, the League for Civil Education, the Lutheran Church of America, Mattachine Society, the Methodist Church, the Methodist Board of Christian Social Concerns, the Methodist Board of Education, *Motive* magazine, the National Council of Churches, the Protestant Episcopal Church, the Tavern Guild of San Francisco, the United Church of Christ, the Young Adult Project, and Youth for Service. Their names are:

Bill Billings	Cleo Glenn	Jan Marinessen	Bill Plath
William Black	Darryl Glied	Del Martin	Walter Press
Roger Burgess	Bob Koch	Ted McIlvenna	Keith Right
Hal Call	Donald Kuhn	John Moore	B. J. Stiles
Robert W. Cromey	Don Lucas	Charles E. Mowry	Guy Strait
Lewis Durham	Orville Luster	C. Kilmer Myers	Billie Talmij
Robert J. Durksen	Phyllis Lyon	Dennis F. Nyberg	Pat Walker
	Dale White		

Dr. Robert L. Treese prepared this article for a Consultation on Theology and the Homosexual, August 12-14, 1966, and revised it in 1973. He is a minister of the United Methodist Church and an Associate Professor of Practical Theology at Boston University's School of Theology.

We were eager to include this article because of its fine scholarship and responsible analysis. Editorially, let us comment that the paper is primarily concerned with Gay men and not Lesbians—appropriately so, since this was the concern of the scriptures as well. Except where otherwise stated, "homosexual" or "gay person" in this article probably refers to a man.

Further, we have retained Treese's use of masculist language. Even in his revision Treese writes out of a church man's experience. We did not wish to violate that relationship of experience and expression.

Finally, we wish Treese had used more Gay sources. We understand why he limited himself primarily to psychological sources: readers are still most open to the testimony and speculation of medical and psychiatric professionals; but because those professionals are often obsessed with determining the "cause" of homosexuality and exploring almost exclusively the genital experience of Gay persons, readers come to think about homosexuality only in these same terms. We are less concerned about what "causes" us, or how titillating or perverted our sexual expression can be made to seem than with the inalterable fact that we do exist and require society's affirmation.

As Gay people we live the lives that professionals in the field of psychology write about only second hand. We are far more expert on the subject of homosexuality than is the moralizing psychiatrist. The professionals themselves may be Gay—as indeed many of them are. We would suggest to these professionals that their contributions would be more credible if they would affirm that they are writing out of their own Gay experiences. "Coming out" would hurt them far less than their closetedness presently hurts their Gay sisters and brothers. Many openly Gay people have written about themselves; we wish Treese had chosen to use more of their material.—Eds.

HOMO-SEXUALITY

A CONTEMPORARY VIEW OF THE BIBLI-CAL PERSPECTIVE

ROBERT L. TREESE

INTRODUCTION

What is God trying to tell us about homosexuality? About sexuality? About creativity and the redemptive community today? These are the questions this paper attempts to face. We are being forced to attend to these questions by

events that we can no longer ignore. The pioneering work of the moral Welfare Council of the Church of England in the early 1950s, which created the
official Committee on Homosexual Offenses and Prostitution in 1954, marked
the end of a long ecclesiastical silence about homosexuality as a recognized
condition of a segment of humanity. The Wolfenden Report[1] challenged the
basic presuppositions of laws regarding homosexual practices, so that on the
third attempt before Parliament the law assigning criminality to homosexual
acts between consenting adults was repealed. The Report also raised inescap-
able theological questions which must be faced now.

In San Francisco, the Council on Religion and the Homosexual evolved
from the faithful and persistent attempts of a few pastors and a few members of the homophile community to communicate with each other. They
sought and achieved common human bases for understanding and fellowship.
The founding of CRH in 1964 is another event which makes it necessary for
us to ask what God may be trying to tell us. CRH has made it possible for
"straight" and "gay" persons to meet one another in mutual trust in search
of mutual acceptance. It has helped us to begin to sense the depth and integrity which exist, actually or potentially, within and among groups of people
who have traditionally written each other off as "pious frauds" or as "per-
verts and sinners."

Two other recent developments serve to force the issue: (1) The Metropolitan Community Church, an organization of Christian gay people, was
begun in 1968 by the Reverend Troy Perry in Los Angeles, and is now a
national movement with some fifty local congregations across the country;
and (2) a new spirit of militancy and dignity is growing among homosexuals.
The Gay Liberation Movement was born out of a crisis in Greenwich Village
in 1969 when a gay bar there, the Stonewall Inn on Christopher Street, was
raided by the police. Instead of passively enduring harassment, as was usual
and expected, a group of homosexuals fought back:

> They were joined by street people and village residents
> in resisting the police, and from the sporadic street
> fighting that lasted three days, the gay liberation move-
> ment emerged . . . . Gay people began to recognize a
> need (after the Stonewall riots) to change the society
> that oppressed us, and to change the image of ourselves
> that society had forced upon us.[2]

In the crisis of the moment the gay militants had found their voice.

In recent years theological wrestlings within the Church have resulted in attempts to view contemporary human experience through a renewed Biblical understanding of God's purposes for the Church and for the rest of the world. These struggles have given us a new awareness of how God has acted and continues to act in and through His creation to bring it to fulfillment. No longer can we think of the Church as the redeemed portion of humanity rescued from a God-forsaken world. We cannot assume now that the work of the Church consists in waiting faithfully and in purity for death and heaven. Nor can we sit by waiting for God to vindicate His righteousness and that of the Church by destroying the world and reconstructing the Kingdom with the people of the Church as His subjects. As Norman DePuy put it in the *American Baptist* magazine:

> There's nobody in the church who is there because
> he's perfect or because he's earned his righteousness.
> He's there because he knows righteousness only comes
> as a gift from God, and that if it were not for God's
> love he'd be in hell. Therefore the church is made up
> of afflicted and sinful people. To call church people
> "straight" is a dangerously loose use of words.[3]

Jesus Christ affirmed human life and showed us that the ultimate test of our love of God, of our commitment to value, lies in our attitudes toward and treatment of other human beings. (See Matthew 25:31-45.) The Church, the community of those who call Him "Lord," far from being in retreat from the world, is thrown into the world to participate in God's continuing reclaiming, restoring, dignifying, humanizing action.

As a churchman, I feel moved to confess that a great deal of the blame for maintaining, if not indeed creating, the fear and guilt surrounding human sexuality in our culture, lies at our feet. The Church has failed to understand and acknowledge sexuality except in terms of reproduction and genitality. This narrow view has relegated sex to the purely physical plane with no regard at all for the deep interpersonal trust and the empathy and love which sexual intercourse, at best, expresses. Of course, the current generation in the Church has somewhat modified these ancient views, but the pall of centuries of sin-obsessed taboos and misanthropic caricatures of human nature still blankets our culture and informs our mores. The mass media's projection of sexuality as experience devoid of relationship and responsibility, as a biological function needing only satiation, and as a means of mass marketing—all this seems to me to be only a result to be expected, the acting out of a degraded view of sex which the Church has helped to foster.

With regard to homosexuality and homosexual practices the Church has maintained a consistent (perhaps because it was unexamined) attitude. Between Thomas Aquinas' designation of homosexuality as *peccatum contra naturum* in the thirteenth century and the developments noted above that began in the 1950s, no theologian, to my knowledge, has seriously examined the nature and meaning of this phenomenon.[4] But the ice has been broken now and perhaps the thaw will continue if enough heat is generated. D. S. Bailey, in England, has done a remarkable study of the historical roots of our attitudes toward homosexuality, and Helmut Thielecke, in Germany, has come out with a forthright opener to theological discussion. Since 1966 when the germ of the present article was first presented as a lecture for the Consultation on Theology and the Homosexual, a large number of books and articles by theologians and churchmen has opened up the question of the Church and the homosexual.[5]

A word of caution and perhaps of reprimand to us is in order at this point. As D. S. Bailey reminds us, we are all in the habit of blaming our favorite whipping boy, the Church, for every attitude or development of which we may disapprove. To be sure the Church is not blameless, but neither is she wholly responsible for the present condition of society. We must see the Church as trying earnestly in each generation, both to conserve values from our tradition—values and tradition from which in part we gain our identity— and to respond openly to new human experience as she attempts to understand God's leading. Sometimes she does the former more effectively than the latter. Naturally her decisions are limited to and by the knowledge and understanding of the time. Thus from our superior position, we should not feel justified in deriding the sixth-century rationale that supported repressive legislation against homosexuals. Homosexual acts were then thought to be responsible for earthquakes, plagues, and other natural disasters. This was the level of knowledge and understanding of causation current in that day. Bailey puts it pungently: "It is not as if throughout the last two millenia reluctant legislators had been forced by the spiritual authority to enact laws and to prescribe punishment which they secretly detested."[6]

We recognize, though, that the medieval attitude of the Church with regard to the question at hand must be challenged and brought up to date. The Church, for all her weakness, can still be an opinion-leader and can still influence culture. At the very least the Church has a responsibility to stay informed.

THE NORMATIVE IMPORTANCE OF THE BIBLE

Before examining specific passages, we need to discuss our stance toward the Bible. We cannot simply write off the Bible as irrelevant. It has helped mold the attitudes of Western civilization. Though grossly abused by many, it is still normative in the life of the Church—that is, it provides the norms, value structure and guidelines for understanding contemporary life and God's purposes for history. It is still influential, though often negatively so, in much of the decision-making of our time.

The typical, unthinking approach to the Bible is that of the literalist, and in varying degrees perhaps we all employ it. This is the approach which says, "That's what it says—and it's God's word, so . . . ." Many homosexuals reject the Bible because they are literalists. Because half a dozen brief passages describe homosexual acts as grievously sinful, they say that the Bible can have no relationship to contemporary life. But to be a literalist one must necessarily be highly selective in the choice of the words which he takes to be God's word. For example, the Old Testament specifically commands that males be circumcised as a sign that they are sons of the covenant. The Christian believes this requirement to be superseded by the new covenant in Christ. But many are not so consistent when dealing, for example, with the Old Testament's Sabbath laws. Instead they apply the elaborate regulation for proper observance of the Sabbath, which is Saturday in the Old Testament, to the Christian Sunday, the Lord's Day, meant to be a day of rejoicing. And they observe those strict regulations even though Jesus said, "The Sabbath was made for man, not man for the Sabbath." Or, as another example, the verse, "Slaves be obedient to those who are your earthly masters" (Ephesians 6:5) used to be taken as God's word in support of the institution of slavery. But the interpretation of other portions of Scripture supported a confluence of political-historical-economic forces which overthrew slavery and caused that verse to be reinterpreted and seen in its proper context. The command that witches should be burned to death was taken at face value in Salem, Massachusetts, and other places until the human spirit was sickened and revolted by the fiendish excesses enacted and until witchcraft was shown by modern science to be a combination of superstition and coincidence. Staunch literalism, then, requires a great lapse in consistency.

An intelligent and workable approach for understanding and appropriating the Bible today affirms that:

(1) The Bible is not the Word of God, but the words of men, in which and through which we believe the living, active, constantly contemporary Word of God comes to men.

(2) A Bible passage is to be interpreted in terms of the experiences, life setting and problems of the specific writer and with respect to the purposes for which it was written.

(3) A passage is to be further explicated in the light of our contemporary experience and knowledge. We must try to see it in relation to our social-psychological-historical-philosophical understanding as well as to our existential knowledge. There may not be agreement, for sometimes—in fact, often—the Bible stands in judgment of our contemporary life, but the task is to discern, as nearly as possible, the meaning for us today.

(4) Although the Bible writers faced the same basic existential questions we face, many of their answers are time-caught, as ours are, and valid only for them. But the values they affirmed by their answers are of significance to us.

(5) The whole Bible is to be seen in light of the Gospel of Jesus Christ and the experience of the early Church.

RELEVANT BIBLICAL PASSAGES

We must consider the Biblical passages which specifically refer to homosexual practices before we attempt to see our problem in the perspective of the Christian faith. There are about a dozen places in the Bible which have been used to support the idea that our current laws and attitudes toward homosexuals are true to "God's law."[7]

Five Instances of Mistranslation

The first five passages we shall consider have been shown to have been mistranslated, errors since corrected in the Revised Standard Version (R.S.V.). In I Kings 14:22-24, 15:12, 22:46; II Kings 23:7, and Deuteronomy 23:17-18 there are references to what was apparently a fertility cult flourishing in the temples. Such cults were more the rule than the exception among primitive peoples. The mysterious forces controlling fertility were propitiated and the utter dependence of man upon its continuation in plant, animal, and human life was expressed by a variety of religious rituals including sacred prostitution. The concept is strange to our ways of thinking, unless we consider for instance the *Playboy* cult, where the values guaranteed by certain rituals are virility and success. The concept then was that the male and female devotees guaranteed the fertility of their crops, their animals and themselves by participating in sexual intercourse with prostitutes who were dedicated to serve the deity in charge of fertility.

> There were prostitutes of either sex within the temple
> in service of the deity. This custom was common and
> recognized everywhere in Phoenician cults and in the
> cults (e.g. of Aphrodite) which were influenced by them.
> The custom was a feature of Canaanite religion and was
> common in Mesopotamia from early times.[8]

The worshipers, by a process of imitative magic, sought to encourage the gods and goddesses to engage in sexual intercourse which was seen as the only way that fertility could be assured.[9]

Bailey has shown that, whereas the King James Version translators correctly rendered the Hebrew noun $Q^e dhesh\bar{a}h$ ("consecrated one") as (female) temple servant (or prostitute), they erred by translating the masculine form of this noun ($Q\bar{a}dh\bar{e}sh$, $Q^e dh\bar{e}sh\bar{\imath}m$, plural) as "sodomite" thinking no doubt that it referred to a male homosexual temple prostitute.[10] They apparently gave no thought to the utter incongruity of homosexual prostitutes serving in a fertility cult. The correct translation is in the R.S.V., "male cult prostitute." His duties, along with those of his female counterpart, were deplored in successive passages. These temple servants were finally banned and their houses destroyed by King Josiah about 625 B.C. (II Kings 23:7, Deuteronomy 23:17-18).

The correction of this error in current translations[11] would not seem worth mentioning except that the King James Version, where the error remains, is still very influential, most especially perhaps with the literalists among us.

Sodom and Gomorrah

This brings us to the Biblical passage which has perhaps been used most to justify our civilization's legal and social abhorrence of homosexuals and homosexual practices. That is the story of the destruction of Sodom and Gomorrah (Genesis 19:1-28). Throughout the centuries, especially in the eras before modern science, and even today among literalists, this story has been used as proof positive that God abhors homosexuality—to such a degree, in fact, that two whole cities were literally destroyed by fire and brimstone from heaven because of it. Recapping the story briefly, God was bent on destroying Sodom and Gomorrah "because the outcry against . . . [them] is great and their sin is very grave," but Abraham importuned Him to first search for as few as ten righteous men who, if found, would justify a change in God's plan (Genesis 18:20-33). So God sent two emissaries, male angels, to Sodom to seek out the righteous, and they lodged for the night in the house of Lot (Abraham's nephew). The "men of Sodom, both young and old, all the people to the last man" (19:4) surrounded Lot's house and demanded that he bring out the visitors "that we may know them" (19:5). When Lot refused, offering them his two daughters instead, they became angry and would have stormed the house had not the angels struck them blind. In the morning, when Lot and his family had fled, the city was utterly destroyed.

The issue lies in the meaning of the *yādhá* (to know). This verb is used alone ten times in the Old Testament to denote sexual intercourse, as in Genesis 4:1: "Now Adam *knew* Eve his wife and she conceived and bore Cain." Bailey points out that this verb is used nine hundred and forty-three times in the Old Testament. In fewer than a dozen of these cases does this word denote coitus and then it unmistakably refers to heterosexual coitus. Another Hebrew verb (*shākhabh*) is used directly to describe "both homosexual and bestial coitus, in addition to that between man and woman." [12] Thus there is no necessity linguistically to see the verb *yādhá* as implying a desire for homosexual acts. In fact, it could well be translated "get acquainted with."

This linguistic argument alone would prove nothing were it not for the fact that the "Old Testament depicts Sodom as a symbol of utter destruction (c.f. Isaiah 13:19; Jeremiah 49:18; 50:40), and its sin as one of such magnitude and scandal as to merit exemplary punishment, but *nowhere does it identify that sin explicitly with the practice of homosexuality.*" [13] Two quotations from the prophets in the sixth century B.C. illustrate this:

> *But in the prophets of Jerusalem I have seen a horrible*
> *thing: they commit adultery and walk in lies; they*
> *strengthen the hands of evildoers, so that no one*
> *turns from his wickedness; all of them have become*
> *like Sodom to me. (Jeremiah 23:14)*

> *Behold, this was the guilt of your sister Sodom: she*
> *and her daughters had pride, surfeit of food, and*
> *prosperous ease, but did not aid the poor and needy.*
> *They were haughty and did* abominable *things before*
> *me; therefore I removed them when I saw it.*
> *(Ezekiel 16:49-50)*

In the latter verses the words "abominable things" could lend themselves to the homosexual interpretation in light of later attitudes toward Sodom, but in the Old Testament "abomination" or "abominable things" is the "conventional term for idolatry." [14]

How did the homosexual interpretation of Sodom's sins originate? Bailey, after thorough study of the writings of the period, finds that the idea began in the second century B.C. in the non-Biblical writings of the Jews. This was the period of Greek ascendency and rule in Palestine. A life-and-death struggle raged for more than two centuries between the more orthodox Jews who did not want Judaism contaminated with Greek ideas and practices, and more liberal Jews who embraced Hellenistic customs and manners. Homosexual practices were among the more objectionable Hellenistic customs eschewed. (Other practices, manners, customs, and so forth in question included habits of dress and speech, athletic activity, architecture, and sculpture. Some Jews went so far as to seek surgery which would remove the scars or marks of circumcision in order to be more Hellenistic.)

Allusions to Sodom's sin as homosexual practices appeared in the late second century B.C.—for example, "that ye become not as Sodom which changed the order of nature" (*Testament of Naphtali*, 3:4-5, ca. 109 B.C.). But the allusions gave way to more explicit expressions in the first century B.C. and

came to full flower in the writings of Philo and Josephus in the first century A.D.
Philo's imagination ran rampant as he described men of Sodom who

> threw off from their necks the law of nature and applied
> themselves to deep drinking of strong liquor and dainty
> feeding and forbidden forms of intercourse. Not only in
> their mad lust for women did they violate the marriages
> of their neighbors, but also men mounted males without
> respect for sex nature which the active partner shares with
> the passive. (De Abrahamo 26:134-136)

Josephus, the Jewish historian and a contemporary of Philo, writes:

> Now when the Sodomites saw the young men [the angels]
> to be of beautiful countenance, and this to an extraordi-
> nary degree . . . they resolved themselves to enjoy those
> beautiful boys by force and violence. (Antiquities I. xi.
> 3:200)

It is significant that the Rabbinical literature, according to Bailey, "reflects
scarcely anything of this development." With the single exception of an allu-
sion to adultery in the Midrash on Genesis, "no sexual (let alone homosexual)
implications can be read into these conceptions [Rabbinical interpretations]
of the sin of Sodom . . . . . Traditionally, the offense of the Sodomites was
supposed to be that of the dog-in-the-manger." It was the early Church Fathers,
taking Philo and other Hellenistic-Jewish writings at face value, who set the
tradition in the Church for the homosexual interpretation of Sodom's destruction. [15]

The significance of this whole disclosure lies in the fact that we cannot, in
truth, say that Sodom proves that God is categorically against homosexuality.
Bailey puts it sharply in the concluding chapter of his important book:

> It has always been accepted without question that God
> declared his judgment upon homosexual practices once
> and for all time by the destruction of the cities of the
> Plain. But Sodom and Gomorrah, as we have seen, actu-
> ally have nothing whatever to do with such practices;
> the interpretation of the Sodom story generally received
> by Western Christendom turns out to be nothing more

> *than a post-Exilic Jewish re-interpretation devised ana*
> *exploited by patriotic rigorists for polemical purposes.*
> *Thus disappears the assumption that an act of Divine*
> *retribution in the remote past has relieved us of the*
> *responsibility for making an assessment of homosexual*
> *acts in terms of theological and moral principles. It is*
> *no longer permissible to take refuge in the contention*
> *that God himself pronounced these acts "detestable*
> *and abominable" above every other sexual sin, nor*
> *to explain natural catastrophes and human disasters*
> *as his vengeance upon those who indulge in them.* [16]

Whether Bailey's conclusions will, in time, gain widespread acceptance is somewhat problematical. So deeply ingrained in our Christianized culture are the traditional exegesis and interpretation that to many persons, even to some homosexuals, Bailey's arguments seem superfluous. The term "sodomy" itself, used variously in common parlance to denote "unnatural" intercourse and in legal proscriptions against such practices, is a constant reminder of the Biblical legend. In recent years some scholars[17] have tended to support Bailey "simply by omitting reference to the homosexual interpretation or by indicating that the sin was that of inhospitality to strangers."[18] Gerhard von Rad, recognizing the fact that Israel always considered Sodom the prime example of depravity in history, is impressed by the testimony of the prophets that the depravity was variously seen as sins of pride, barbarity, adultery, hardheartedness or prosperous ease. Nevertheless, he appears to accept the homosexual interpretation and tries to conjecture how the story may have been given its present form. [19] John H. Marks, in *The Interpreter's One-Volume Commentary on the Bible*, takes the cautious if somewhat ambivalent position of von Rad;[20] even this is a welcome change from *The Interpreter's Bible* (Vol. 1, 1952), which poses no alternative to the traditional exegesis.

It is apparent that Bailey has suggested a way of understanding the Sodom incident which is convincingly more true to prophetic and rabbinical interpretations than was the later Christian tradition. Biblical scholars can no longer, with impunity, ignore the issues he raised. But the problem continues in new translations and revisions which maintain the translation of *yādhá* in homosexual terms. The New English Bible, for example, renders it "have intercourse

with." The Jerusalem Bible has a more ambiguous "abuse them," but an exegeti-
cal footnote removes the ambiguity with "the unnatural vice that takes its
name from this incident . . . and was punished by death."

We must not allow ourselves to forget that the traditional and, for centuries unquestioned, interpretation of the sin of Sodom supported the tradition
in Christian nations of legislating death for male homosexual acts. Such laws
were in force for centuries. In England, for instance, capital punishment for
sodomy was not eliminated until 1861.

The Six Specific References

With the mistranslated Sodom passages accounted for, there are six passages
in the Bible which explicitly designate homosexual practices as gross sins, five
dealing with males and one with females. These can neither be ignored nor explained away, but they can be put in perspective. It may be well to point out
at the outset that the Bible shows no knowledge of homosexuality *per se*; it
knows nothing of the condition of homosexuality as distinct from heterosexuality, the complexity of human sexuality, or the possible causes of sexual
variance. All the references are to homosexual acts, not to the enduring homosexual identity, as gross sins.

The two references in the Old Testament are in the Levitical Holiness Code,
the codification of laws for maintaining the covenant through spiritual, ritual,
and ceremonial purity and separation from other peoples. Leviticus 18:22 is
imbedded in a long passage proscribing incest, intercourse during menstruation,
adultery, bestiality, and incongruously on the surface, child sacrifice. It reads,
"You shall not lie with a male as with a woman; it is an abomination."

Leviticus 20:13 likewise comes in the midst of a passage repeating essentially the same list of grievous sins, but specifying the death penalty rather than
exile for those who commit the immoralities of child sacrifice, incest, adultery,
homosexual acts, and bestiality: "If a man lies with a male as with a woman,
both of them have committed an abomination; they shall be put to death,
their blood is upon them."

Two issues are raised by these very specific statements about homosexual
acts between males. First, the fact that homosexual acts appear in a list of
offenses which are attributed to Egypt ("where you dwell") and Canaan ("to
which I am bringing you"), and are considered an "abomination" raises the

question of underlying meaning. Bailey discusses the word "abomination"
(Tō'ēbhāh) in this perspective:

> Research fails to establish any satisfactory positive
> support for the allegation that homosexual practices were
> customary among the nations surrounding the Hebrews . . .
> it is not impossible that the attribution in question
> [i.e. of homosexual practices in Egypt and Canaan] is
> simply a piece of rhetorical denigration . . . designed
> to intensify Israel's sense of national "holiness" or
> separation as a peculiar people dedicated to Yahweh.
> Supposing this to be the case, it would seem that the
> significance of Tō'ēbhāh (abomination) in these verses
> has often been misunderstood. This term, as we have
> seen, is closely associated with idolatry and designates
> not only false gods but also the worship and conduct
> of those who serve them. By a natural extension of
> meaning, however, it can also denote whatever reverses
> the proper order of things and this seems to be the
> connotation (of abomination in these verses) . . . .
> Such acts are regarded as an "abomination" not . . .
> because they were practiced by Egyptian or Canaanite
> idolators (for of this there is no proof) but because,
> as a reversal of what is sexually natural, they exem-
> plify the spirit of idolatry which is itself the funda-
> mental subversion of true order . . . . They (these
> laws) condemn homosexual acts . . . between males
> as typical expressions of the ethos of heathenism
> which Israel must renounce no less than religious
> and cultural syncretism with the nations which bow
> down to idols.[21]

Until proved wrong by Hebrew scholars, this interpretation is stimulating to
me. The Holiness Code sought to fence out the alien world and to establish rules
for the separation (holiness) of the People of God. Seen in this light, homosexual acts then are proscribed because they are associated with idolatry, the re-
versal of the true order. At this juncture, we note that the inclusion in the lists

of child sacrifice is not incongruous after all, but rather tends to support this interpretation of a proscription of idolatry. This leads directly to the second issue raised by these passages.

For the Christian, the Jewish legal code has been superseded by the Gospel of Jesus Christ. As Thielicke suggests, "It would never occur to anyone to wrench these laws of cultic purification from their concrete situation and give them the kind of normative authority that the Decalogue, for example, has." [22] We tend to deal with the Holiness Code selectively, rejecting all instructions no longer relevant: those for animal sacrifice, for instance; and all injunctions regarding ritual purification, such as those to follow childbirth, menstruation, the handling of anything dead, etc.; as well as all dietary laws such as eating flesh with blood in it. We accept as consistent with the Christian Gospel any of the admonitions against behavior which causes harm or abuse to another human being or dishonors God. The Gospel freed man from the Law, and this becomes the criterion for understanding the behavior codes. To accept Leviticus 20:13 (that those guilty of homosexual acts should be put to death) and to reject, for example, Leviticus 20:25 ("You shall therefore make a distinction between the clean beast and the unclean"), or Leviticus 20:27 ("A man or woman who is a medium or a wizard shall be put to death, they shall be stoned with stones"), is inconsistency of the rankest sort, to say the least. But we are still left with the problem of homosexuality and homoerotic acts as they may be seen in light of the Gospel. We will discuss this problem in a later section.

Probably the best known New Testament verses on our subject are Romans 1:26-27:

> *26 For this reason God gave them up to dishonorable passions. Their women exchanged natural relations for unnatural*
>
> *27 and the men likewise gave up natural relations with women and were consumed with passion for one another, men committing shameless acts with men and receiving in their own persons the due penalty for their error.*

It should be noted that, while verse 26 does not unambiguously refer to lesbianism (the "unnatural relations" could be with a male partner), when taken in the context of verse 27 along with the adverb "likewise" (*homoiōs,* in like manner) it is doubtless to be so interpreted. Verse 26 thus is the only reference in Scripture to female homosexual acts.

The passage in which these verses are imbedded (1:18-31) contains Paul's discussion of why man (he seems to be referring specifically to Gentiles, that is, non-Jews) does not know God or does not live as though God exists. Even without any special revelation, as that granted to the Jews, Gentiles, he states, should be able to acknowledge the Creator in the very facts of Creation: "Ever since the creation of the world his invisible nature, his eternal power and deity, has been clearly perceived in the things that have been made" (vs. 20). He goes on to say that man who refuses to honor God turns instead to "images resembling mortal man or birds or animals or reptiles (thus God has abandoned them) . . . to the dishonoring of their bodies among themselves, because they exchanged the truth about God for a lie and worshipped and served the creature rather than the Creator" (vss. 23-25). Then follow the verses which concern us: this would-be-autonomous man's refusal to accept his creatureliness by honoring the Creator is exemplified by disorders in the natural relationships of man to woman among them. "Because the lower and the higher, the creature and the Creator, are exchanged ('perverted') the result is a perverse supremacy of the inferior desires over the spirit."[23]

Again, basic to the meaning of this passage is the normal Jewish concept that sees "the root cause of both sin and corruption in idolatry."[24] Paul lists both sensual sins (vss. 24-27) and anti-social sins (vss. 28-31) as the evidence of God's judgment against idolatry. The latter list, more universally indicting, includes covetousness, malice, deceit, envy, murder, strife, gossip, insolence, boastfulness, etc.—a list which points up dramatically the real peril and fruits of idolatrous behavior. The phrase "God gave them up to . . ." in verses 24, 26 and 28, as Gerald Cragg points out,

> *emphasizes the judicial nature of the process (of judgment) . . . . This is the way in which the laws of the moral universe inevitably work. The punishment of sin lies not in any direct intervention by which God disciplines offenders, but in the consequences which naturally follow from a lawless life. As it has been incisively remarked by Charles Gore, "The wages of sin is also its fruit."*[25]

Both the sensual and the anti-social sins are idolatrous because they indicate exclusive delight and ultimate concern for the creature and for created things: thus the sins themselves become false gods.

Getting back to the verses which most concern us here, two points must be made. First, Paul could just as well have chosen other examples of sensual idolatry as a means of illustrating the distortions of the Creator's purposes by man's willful refusal to acknowledge his own creaturehood, for Paul's purpose here is to point out "the hidden connections between the Fall, as a disordering of creation, and the pathological changes in existence in the world as a whole." [26] He is obviously discussing original sin ("Therefore God gave them up in the lusts of their hearts to impurity" [vs. 24]) as exemplified by specific acts contrary to the Creator's purposes. It is important at this point to bear in mind that Paul is talking about concrete libidinous acts of a homosexual nature, and is not discussing the predisposition to homosexuality. Nor is he leaving room for the possibility that homosexual persons can acknowledge and honor the Creator. But the theological issue that concerns us lies not in the concrete acts, but in the meaning and possibilities of the homosexual condition, as an empirical fact in relation to God's order of creation. It would have been out of place for Paul to have discussed this issue in this context, even had he known of the reality of variance as opposed to perversion. It is true, though, that such knowledge would have undoubtedly caused him to select other illustrations of sensual idolatry.

As will be discussed later in a section on causation, if it is true that sexual variance is a reality and that homosexual orientation and behavior naturally emerge from that reality, then to speak of homoerotic acts as "unnatural" in all cases is illogical. To be sure, it is asking too much to expect Paul to have twentieth-century knowledge and outlook on this matter. But we can understand perversion of the natural in this case to mean homosexual acts by heterosexually oriented persons or heterosexual acts by homosexually oriented persons.

At this point, one is moved on reflection to question the implication in these verses that every homoerotic act is, by definition, a gross idolatrous sin. Here we encounter the second central issue deriving from these passages. As human beings we share a common sinfulness in the expression of our sexuality for we respond to the impulses of both lust and love; sexuality can be an instrument of either. Paul's insight that "all have sinned and fall short of the glory of God" (Romans 3:23) applies to mankind's sometimes vain efforts to fulfill and control sexual feelings, as well as to the other dimensions of being. For the Christian, responsible sexual relationships are the expression of deep and abiding love. They enhance the integrity of persons, and are characterized by self-giving and fidelity. To the degree that redemption is experienced, the Christian is enabled, by the Grace of God, to overcome the exploitive, utilitarian aspects of sexuality and to move toward a relationship in which each person respects and honors the other and which is a profound expression of abiding love. The implication in the verses under consideration is that this quality of love is possible only between persons of heterosexual identity. Pondering this, one sees it is patently ridiculous, for it denies personhood and integrity to an entire segment of humanity.

It must not be supposed from anything that has been said up to this point that Paul was not rejecting homosexual acts. In I Corinthians 6:9-10 he includes them in a catalogue of unrighteous practices which will deny the Kingdom of God to persons guilty of such offenses:

> Do not be deceived: neither the immoral [pornois—
> lit. "fornicators"], nor idolators, nor adulterers, nor
> homosexuals, nor thieves, nor the greedy, nor drunkards,
> nor revilers, nor robbers will inherit the kingdom of God.

It is very misleading and unfortunate indeed, as Bailey has pointed out,[27] that the translators of the Revised Standard Version, now so widely used in our land, have elected to replace two separate Greek words denoting homosexual practices with one English word which can only mean all persons of homosexual predisposition, masking the distinction between them. The translation does not make possible the identification of libidinous practices on a par with adultery. The meaning is obvious in the Greek text, where *malakoi* (meaning in this context "effeminate" or "the passive male partners") and *arsenokoitai* (referring to the active males in the homosexual acts, sometimes also being rendered simply as "sodomites") are used to refer to specific homosexual practices. But it is clear that again Paul is speaking of such acts, without qualification, as being seriously sinful.

It is of interest to note that Paul, either in writing *from* (Romans), or *to* Corinth, is responding to a city where licentiousness was apparently "the name of the game." One can not but agree with Paul that the carnival promiscuity and orgies implied in this passage, along with other person-destroying behavior, would not be characteristic of those who earnestly seek after the Kingdom. I discussed this passage with a mature Christian gay person who led me to deeper insight by affirming that Paul was right in proscribing licentiousness, but warning that these verses should not be seen as referring to a mature union between two men or two women who genuinely love and honor each other. Licentiousness is not to be equated with homosexual love.

A similar catalogue of grievous sinners for whom the law was made is in I Timothy 1:9-10:

> 9 *that the law is not laid down for the just but for the lawless and disobedient, for the ungodly and sinners, for the unholy and profane, for murderers of fathers, and murderers of mothers, for manslayers,*
>
> 10 *immoral persons* [pornois, *lit. "fornicators"*] *sodomites, kidnappers, liars, perjurers, and whatever else is contrary to sound doctrine.*

Summary of Biblical Evidence

The two Old Testament verses (Leviticus 18:22 and 20:13) are historically interesting but have no contemporary relevance because of their setting in the rules for cultic purification, and because of the lack of clarity in their underlying meaning. The Sodom story has been shown to have been used fallaciously because of mistranslation and rigid tradition in condemnation of homosexuality. But the four verses cited from the New Testament (Romans 1:26, 27; I Corinthians 6:10, and I Timothy 1:10) indicate with no possibility of qualification that homosexual practices were considered by Paul (and the writer of I Timothy) to be concrete sins on a par with adultery and murder, and evidence of the original sin with which the human race is infected. Thus the moral question has been illuminated somewhat, but a theological stance on the issue of homosexual identity is not explored in the New Testament. We now turn to a tentative investigation of this theological question.

A LARGER BIBLICAL VIEW OF HOMOSEXUALITY

We must begin this section by setting the context for theological discussion from two perspectives: (1) we must consider the definition and the "causes" of homosexuality; and (2) we must meditate on the meaning of my own personal knowledge of homosexuals, since theological reflection, to be true to its essential nature, must be grounded in contemporary phenomena and knowledge.

Most people who have given any thought to the problems of definition and "causality" are aware of the vast sea of confusion into which this leads. Everyone seems to have an opinion on causation, from the extremes of "I (He) was born this/that way" to "My (His) mother made me (him) this/that way." From genetics, to psychodynamics, to social-cultural conditioning, theorists run the gamut. We might be able to glean some truth from all these approaches. But most of the research and writing in this field has been done by psychoanalysts, psychiatrists, anthropologists, psychologists and sociologists; some recent studies have been done by theologians. In the midst of much continuing hard work the confusion seems to be settling into definable patterns which give us some guidance on these basic problems. The book *Sexual Inversion: the Multiple Roots of Homosexuality*, edited by Dr. Judd Marmor, Clinical Professor of Psychiatry at the University of California at Los Angeles, [28] brings a great deal of order into the chaos and offers refreshing analyses of the current state of various theories. Dr. Marmor's introduction to this anthology is a frank and open-ended critique of current views of homosexuality and it will be helpful to lean heavily in this section on what appears to be the most comprehensive attempt to put homosexuality in perspective as a human phenomenon.

We can discern certain distinct categories of homoerotic practices: There is the true homosexual for whom heterosexual experience is not desirable. There are those who engage in transitory homosexual acts because of enforced deprivation of heterosexual outlets over long periods of time (prisoners and military personnel, for example). There are those who engage because of rebellion or hostility, or for money and status (as, for example, the young male prostitutes, many of whom have little homosexual predisposition).[29] There is the adolescent experimentation with which many are personally familiar. A definition of homosexuality must "exclude patterns of homosexual behavior that are not motivated by specific, preferential desire," says Dr. Marmor and he therefore defines the homosexual as

> *one who is motivated, in adult life, by a definite prefer-*
> *ential erotic attraction to members of the same sex and*
> *who usually (but not necessarily) engages in overt sexu-*
> *al relations with them.*[30]

Here the significant phrase is "definite preferential erotic attraction," with its implication that the patterns of behavior are part of the personality structure of the individual and that the desire is the same, even when a heterosexual alternative is present.

This means then that an individual having a "definite preferential erotic attraction to members of the same sex" may in all respects but this one be very much like any other individual who has a "definite preferential erotic attraction" to members of the opposite sex. The common tendency to stereotype all homosexuals on the basis of the extreme or bizarre behavior of some is a cultural prejudice, the nonsense of which becomes obvious if we make the equally absurd assumption that all heterosexuals are alike, or that they are to be judged by the most bizarre behavior of any heterosexual. Dr. Marmor develops this thought further:

> *One reflection of this stereotyping is the almost univer-*
> *sal belief that homosexuals are not to be trusted with*
> *young people of the same sex. The assumption that*
> *they are somehow less in control of their impulses than*
> *are heterosexuals is the same kind of assumption that*
> *underlines white prejudice against Negroes or native-*
> *born prejudice against foreigners. In all these instances,*
> *the feeling is a reflection of fear based on lack of inti-*
> *mate knowledge of the people involved. A homosexual*
> *individual is neither more nor less trustworthy, necessari-*
> *ly, with young people of the same sex than a hetero-*
> *sexual is trustworthy with young people of the opposite*
> *sex.*[31] *[A 1972 study in Oregon indicated over 95% of*
> *child molestation offenses to be heterosexual contacts,*
> *mostly within the family unit—uncles and stepfathers.—Eds.]*

Without sacrificing the force of this claim that there is no "homosexual personality" *per se*, Marmor qualifies the above statement. He reminds us that, because of the extreme pressures of a society which makes the homosexual's "behaviour *ipso facto* maladaptive," he tends "statistically (to be) more likely to feel inadequate and to show evidence of less adequate ego formation" than the heterosexual:

> *There is, nevertheless, as wide a personality variation*
> *among homosexuals as among heterosexuals: from*
> *extremely passive to extremely aggressive ones; from*
> *quiet introverts to loud and raucous extroverts; from*
> *hysterics to compulsives; from sexually inhibited and*
> *timid types to sexually promiscuous and self-flaunting*
> *ones; from irresponsible sociopaths to highly responsible*
> *and law-abiding citizens.* [32]

Marmor's judgment that there is no "homosexual personality" *per se* is supported by the research of Evelyn Hooker who in 1957 published a study in which sixty men, thirty homosexual and thirty heterosexual, matched by age, education and intelligence, were given a battery of projective tests. The test materials, along with extensive life histories, were analyzed by psychologists independent of the study. The analysts were unable to distinguish the homosexuals from the heterosexuals; nor did they find significant evidence of pathology in the homosexual profiles. Dr. Hooker concluded from the study that

> *homosexuality as a clinical entity does not exist. Its*
> *forms are as varied as are those of heterosexuality.*
> *Homosexuality may be a deviation in sexual patterns*
> *which is in the normal range, psychologically.* [33]

With regard to "causality," the origins of homosexuality are seen now to be multi-factorial, including sociocultural, psychodynamic, biological, and situational elements. "There is yet no single constellation of factors that can adequately explain all homosexual deviations." [34]

Continuing research has failed to reveal much consistent evidence of a genetic origin, of either a chromosomal abnormality or hormone differentiation, which could solve the mystery of causation. [35] In fact, the more I study the issue, the more mysterious I find the causes of heterosexuality to be as well.

In contemporary discussions of homosexuality there are apparently two major constellations of suggested solutions to the problem of origins. These can be classified roughly as the "sickness" group (endorsed by many psychotherapists) and the "sociocultural" group (endorsed primarily by social psychiatrists and sociologists).

The claim that all homosexual persons are *ipso facto* mentally ill, on the basis of data from therapeutic sessions, is at the very least open to question. Marmor is refreshing and a bit unusual in my experience when he considers the question of whether homosexuality is, as such, a sickness. He states with remarkable and welcome candor that

> *the concepts of psychoanalysts are all derived from the*
> *study of homosexuals who have sought psychoanalytic*
> *therapy or else have been referred by external difficulties . . .*
> *a strong possibility thus exists that traditional psycho-*
> *analytic concepts about the characteriological defects*
> *of homosexuals are based on a skewed sampling of*
> *homosexuals and may not accurately represent the*
> *spectrum of personalities present in the total homosexual*
> *population . . . . If the judgments of pyschoanalysts*
> *about heterosexuals were based only on those they see*
> *as patients, would they not have the same skewed impres-*
> *sion of heterosexuals as a group?* [36] *[I.e., that they are*
> *all sick. —Eds.]*

The sociocultural viewpoint postulates that sexual expression is a learned response. That is, there is some evidence that sexuality operates adaptively, that at birth a human being is psychosexually neutral and this potential "permits the development and perpetuation of divers patterns of psycho-sexual orientation and functioning in accordance with the life experience each individual may encounter and transact." [37] The human being—unlike animals lower on the evolutionary scale which have complex inherited patterns of instincts subject to little manipulation by the environment—is born "not with complex instinctual patterns, but with relatively unfocused basic biological drives. The direction these drives take in human beings and the objects to which they become attached are subject to enormous modifications by learning." [38] This means that a human being at birth has what Martin Hoffman calls "an undifferentiated sexual potential" [39] and that the direction the sex drives take is determined significantly by positive and negative learning gained from the environment. Marmor goes so far as to affirm that on the basis of research by Money and by Hampson and Hampson into the origins of sexual behavior and gender role, "the objects of human sexual drives are experientially determined rather than biologically determined." And he concludes, on this basis

> that there is nothing inherently "unnatural" about life
> experiences that predispose an individual to a preference
> for homosexual object-relations, except insofar as this
> preference represents a socially condemned form of
> behavior in our culture and consequently carries with
> it certain sanctions and handicaps.[40]

Herein lies a serious problem we have yet to face, if the above be true. The learning apparently takes place very subtly and very early:

> Gender identity and lust orientation are quite possibly
> imprinted, perhaps nearly irrevocably, by the end of
> the child's twenty-fourth month, though research is not
> yet conclusive. If after that time the child's environment
> or family setting were radically changed before he had
> developed adult coping mechanisms, there would be
> grave danger of creating a permanently unstable adult.
> Thus, if a homosexual orientation were imprinted,
> unless child analysis could be secured, it would be better
> to allow the child to develop into a healthy homosexual,
> as many do. One reason, perhaps, that we see so many
> maladjusted homosexuals arises simply from our phobic
> social attitude toward same-sex learning cues: we too
> often officially encourage heterosexual object-choice,
> but fail to realize that a homosexual object-choice has
> been imprinted.[41]

All this suggests that we may truly be dealing with sickness, but that society, not the homosexual, is the patient.

At this point in time I am led to conclude that the impulses of both homosexuality and heterosexuality seem to develop quite unconsciously and that we emerge as one or the other, or some combination of both, quite apart from any conscious act of will or desire.

The theological issues were raised inevitably and abruptly for me when I
began working with homosexuals on projects of common concern. I came to
this experience with naive acceptance of the cultural norm of heterosexuality
and its accompanying attitudes—ignorance of and condescension to homosexuality—rejecting the idea of what I considered to be perversion (with, however,
no conscious rejection of the homosexual person). But I was suddenly faced
with the realization that something didn't add up. Life isn't that neat and
simple.

I have seen "gay" persons accept Christ and join His body. Was grace with-
held? This same question was raised by the elders of Jerusalem when they had
Peter on the carpet for baptizing Cornelius, a Gentile. He had been amazed when
the Holy Spirit had directed him to the home of a non-Jew and had likewise
prepared Cornelius for his message. "Truly," he said, "I perceive that God
shows no partiality, but in every nation anyone who fears him and does what
is right is acceptable" (Acts 19:34-35). In Peter's experience I see a parallel to
my own. The question comes in Peter's phrase "does what is right." Is it possible, I had to ask myself, that homosexuality can be "right" for some persons?

I have come to know and admire some mature and responsible homosexual
people. They have fought through God-knows-what-kind-of-Hell in the identity-
formation crisis, and still face daily the threat of the ruination of their lives—
the loss of jobs and social standing—if their true natures become known to
employers and authorities. Yet these persons are committed to relationships
which are fulfilling. The plumbline of judgment must be my own perception
of the capacity of these persons for openness to other human beings, for
mature and responsible social involvements, and for love in its fulfilling depth.
I must in the face of the church's "no" speak a loud "yes" to these persons,
for I have seen the marks of self-giving Christian love upon their lives.

With these two contemporary perspectives in mind—current definitions and
theories of causality, and my admittedly subjective (but not therefore invalid)
experience—I turn finally to ask questions of our theology and to propose
tentative guidelines for a theology which includes the phenomenon under consideration.

The Creation of Man

> So God created man in his own image, in the image of
> God he created him; male and female he created them.
> (Genesis 1:27)

That man was created male and female, in the image of God, raises at once the question of the meaning of obvious physical sex differentiation and what has been taken as inevitably concomitant, the psycho-sexual expression of his sex differentiation. Are male and female the same ontologically? The Hebrews believed that a man was incomplete without a woman and children. The good life was the family life; barrenness was a curse. (This may explain the extremity of punishment for persons involved in homosexual practices in Leviticus 20: 13). They thus affirmed the unity that sex difference and differences in psycho-sexual expression represented; this idea is very much a part of the Judeo-Christian view of man. Without in the least belittling the ontological reality of this unity, we must ask the question, "Does this fit all of the facts? " Does it, in fact, define the essential nature of man? Thielicke discusses this unity as follows:

> The differentiation of the sexes is so constitutive of
> humanity *that, first, it appears as a primeval order (Gen. 1:*
> *27; 2:18ff) and endures as a constant despite its deprava-*
> *tion in the Fall (Gen. 3:16), and, second, that* to it is
> attributed symbolic value for the fundamental structure
> of all human existence, *that is to say, for the existence*
> *of man in his relationship to his fellow man, for the fact*
> *that he is defined by his being as a Thou in relationship*
> *to a Thou.* [42]

It is apparent to me that perceptive as this statement is, it nevertheless errs by equating biological (and perhaps psychological) sex differentiation with essential being. Thielicke sees sex distinctions as having "symbolic value for the fundamental structure of all human existence." He qualifies this idea by further stating that this means a man's relationship to his fellow man defines him as a man. This is to affirm the ontological unity of biological sex difference and psycho-sexual expressions—that is, it is to insist that such unity is inherent in the creation of man and therefore defines man as made in the image of God.

Thielicke may not have taken all facts into account. Male-and-female at birth may be no more than a physical differentiation (allowing every possibility as in the eventual kind of sexual relationship which may develop). The potentiality for sexual expression may simply be an undifferentiated potential at birth, and the direction which the sex drive takes in seeking expression—the

choice of another human being to which the drive shall ultimately be attached·
—may be truly conditioned by learning. The "differentiation of the sexes" may
not be so "constitutive of humanity" as Thielicke assumes.

The crucial question is also implied by Thielicke. This is the question of
relationship, what he calls "a Thou in relationship to a Thou." He approving-
ly quotes Barth, who says that "man does not have the choice to be fellow-
human or something else . . . Man exists in this differentiation, in this duali-
ty." [43] Barth is affirming here the ultimate significance of sex differentiation.
With the first part of Barth's statement I could not be more in agreement.
Certainly man is defined by his relationship—he has no choice but to be "fellow-human." But must the "fellow-human" be in relationship to a "fellow-
human" of the opposite sex? The theological norm would correctly be seen
as "fellow-human relationship." But there is a good possibility, given the current theories of sexual nature as noted above, that man should be defined in
relationship to "fellow man" strictly as a Thou in relationship to a Thou and
not by biological differentiation or sexual relationship. [44]

Thus I must conclude that man in the image of God, in the manward
sense, means that the individual is incomplete apart from responsible relationships with an other, in community; in the Godward sense it means ultimately
that each person finally stands alone in "unmediated relationship before God." [45]

When we speak of man's essential nature and his essential relationship to
God in the eschatological dimension (that is, in accordance with the ultimate
intention of God) sex differentiation is of little importance. In support of this
unqualified aloneness before God, this "unmediated relationship" as the meaning of man being made in God's image, recall Jesus' statement that "They
neither marry nor are given in marriage" in the Kingdom of God (Mark 12:25);
and note that Paul, thinking in eschatological terms, completely separated sexuality from life (I Corinthians 7:1ff); and said "there is neither male nor female,
for you are all one in Christ Jesus" (Galatians 3:28).

On the Fall and Original Sin

The second account of creation (Genesis 2:4-3:24) contains the story of Adam
and Eve and the act of disobedience which eventuated in what theologians call
the Fall of Man. By this myth is explained a fundamental fact of human experience: there is a tragic contradiction between man's essence and his existence,
between what man senses he was meant to be and what he is. The myth affirms

the Creator's good intent, and the creature's perversion of that intent. It recognizes the essential estrangement of man from his Creator, and hence from other men and even from self. Such a myth is a necessity to capture and personify the existential longings for purpose and meaning and relationship in life, and the pervasive quality of paradox in man's existence. For example, his capacity for goodness is equalled by his capacity for evil, and his freedom is limited by his willingness to be bound. This is not the place to discuss the merits of the concept of the Fall except to say that it is not to be interpreted biologically to mean we inherit from one man and woman our sinful natures. Nor is it necessarily to be assumed that any such ideal state existed in history from which men have fallen.[46] Rather, it is every man's story—illustrating the Creator's intent and every man's distortion of that intent.

From the perspective of the Fall and the concept of original sin—that is, estrangement and assumed independence of creature from Creator—one can view both homosexuality and heterosexuality as perversions of the original or intended order of nature, insofar as both are conditions caused by human sin. This would serve to explain the sociocultural determinants of our sexual behavior, which are the result of generations of ignorance, of outdated taboos, of a too-narrow view of life, and of a cumulative social fabric of sins against the deviant—society as the patient, as it were. It also explains the social-psychological conditioning (also cumulative) which occurs in the family, and which can distort human personality unknowingly. But if homosexuality were found to be genetically determined then this explanation would not serve at all. When we ask why evil exists, we can account for moral evil (sin) as resulting from man's free choice and deliberate acts (which may have cumulative social-psychological effects). But we must also face the fact that natural evil exists—congenital deformity, to name one example. Such evil must be seen as either works of the devil, or some other personification of evil at war with God; as deliberate acts of God, hence not ultimately evil; as evidence of the existence of an as yet "uncreated chaos" over which the Creator has not yet assumed control; or as part of the statistical chance the Creator must take in His working to bring His Creation to perfection.

It would appear that men of any and every sexual persuasion are all equally under condemnation of the Fall—the inevitable distortion of the Creator's intention. Thielicke is certainly correct when he says:

> *There is not the slightest excuse for maligning the*
> *constitutional homosexual morally or theologically. We*
> *are all under the same condemnation (original sin, the*
> *guilt of which and fact of which we all participate in)*
> *and each of us has received his "share" of it. In any*
> *case, from this point of view the homosexual's share of*
> *that condemnation has no greater gravity which would*
> *justify any Pharasaic feeling of self-righteousness and*
> *integrity on the part of "normal" persons.* [47]

The Thou-Thou Relationship

It was argued in a previous section that the current ontological doctrine which affirms that man's existence as man, in fact that which makes him human, is "his being as a Thou in relationship to a Thou," that is, in relationship to another human being. We took issue with the claim that sex differentiation, even as a symbol, is fundamental to the structure of this relationship. Now in Genesis 2:24 this question comes sharply before us once more:

> *Therefore a man leaves his father and his mother and*
> *cleaves to his wife, and they become one flesh.*

We are moved to reflect on the central significance of this verse for the Christian concept of marriage, and upon Jesus' use of it in Mark 10:7-8 where he adds, "What therefore God has joined together, let not man put asunder" (v. 9). Marriage is seen as ordained and blessed by God. Implicit here are the values, in an agrarian culture, for the stability, the generativity, and the sexual control of the monogamous family. But Christian marriage is more than this. Christian marriage is a relationship of fidelity and love in which the individuals may grow in grace, in which *agape* may develop as true self-giving. It is impossible for me to see Christian marriage apart from relationship to the Body of Christ. For me Christian marriage is sacramental, a relationship in Christ which truly is a means of grace.

Christian marriage, then, is more than sexual union. Certainly more is implied by "one flesh" than this, though it is an important constituent. Rather, the sexual union must be seen as the expression of a relationship of mutual love, of empathy, of confidentiality, and of trust. There is little evidence that heterosexual union can *produce* these qualities of relationship, but there is much evidence that such union does serve to symbolize, enact, express, and enhance such qualities already existent. Cannot a union of homosexual persons also serve to symbolize, enact, express, and even enhance qualities of relationship already existent? I think so. I have known a number of homosexual couples who have developed highly successful relationships over relatively long periods of time, one of twenty-five years' duration and several of more than ten years. The sociocultural and psychological pressures on homosexuals account for the difficulty some have in establishing permanent relationships comparable to the marriage of heterosexuals. Recall Marmor's conclusion that in all ways, save one, homosexuals exhibit as wide a range of personality variation as heterosexuals do, and that the tendency "to feel less adequate and to show evidence of less adequate ego formation" is inevitable in a society which proscribes every manifestation of the sexual nature with which they have been endowed.[48] Thielicke recognizes that grave hazards face the homosexual and thus make permanent relationships more difficult to achieve; but the difficulties do not imply that such relationships are less desirable than they are for heterosexuals. I quote this long passage for its magnificent description of the problem:

> 1. The homosexual does not have the benefit of living with a supportive order that is informed by a traditional ethos such as that of the institution of marriage. Instead of having at his disposal a set of prefabricated decisions which are made for him by the tradition and make it easier for him to find his way about, he is to an unimaginably greater degree thrown back upon himself. Since he generally begins only gradually to recognize his disposition, he goes through phases of terrible loneliness and stages of groping and uncertain improvisations.
>
> 2. Otherwise than in the "normal sphere," the non-ingrained normative attitude easily produces a propensity toward the excessive, toward rapidly changing partnerships (promiscuity) and thus a sabotage of even that relative "order" which the homosexual could achieve on his basis.
>
> 3. The ostracism the homosexual suffers through the criminal law and the defensive instinct of society leads

him to frequent very dubious circles. He cannot risk any
public attempt to make advances. Whereas the "normal"
person is permitted to regard a representative of the other
sex as a potential partner and is exposed only to the pos-
sibility of being refused (without thereby being socially or
morally compromised), the homosexual runs the danger
of encountering a "normal" person, with all the consequen-
ces that this may involve. This search for a partner of his
own kind in the shady areas of society means an extra-
ordinarily heavy spiritual burden and, what is more, a
dangerous temptation especially for the person who really
wants to live an ethically responsible life.

4. The same burden and temptation result from the
fact that the homosexual must wear a mask and act like
a hypocrite before friends and acquaintances, and as a
rule even in his own family, but nevertheless live in con-
stant fear of discovery and its consequent compromise of
character. Thus he is thrown into a situation of perma-
nent conflict. [49]

Even if two people of the same sex are fortunate enough to find one another and seek to create a mutually responsible, permanent relationship of fidelity
and trust and love, they are still plagued by public censure if they live together, and are considered criminals (in most states) if they express their affection
and fidelity sexually.

At the Consultation on Theology and the Homosexual in San Francisco in
1966, it was refreshing to hear homosexual couples speak of the quality of
personally fulfilling relationships which some of them had achieved (and which
others longed for) when the persistently elusive fidelity and mutual trust were
attained. They were seeking some ethical guidelines by which to pattern their
relationships. Some felt that imitation of heterosexual marriage was not particularly desirable because the homophile "marriage" is more nearly one between two equals, and because the record of fulfilling heterosexual marriages
is not too spectacular. Without ethical guides, they said, they fall back on
kindness and fidelity, and a pledge not to misuse one another. Others made it
clear that the permanent relationship was "the authenticating force in our lives"

and that they were guided by that which brings the other to fulfillment as a person.

Logically and theologically, are there any reasons why we cannot in good conscience explore the possibilities and means of encouraging such relationships between mature homosexual couples? Further, is there any theological reason why the Church cannot bless the union of a homosexual couple in Christ?

One must not, it seems to me, unthinkingly use the term "marriage" for such a union. All the argument above indicates that I affirm Christian marriage to be a quality of relationship in Christ, regardless of the sex of the two partners. Nevertheless the term "marriage" also has profound legal and cultural meanings and implies an aspect of control. Marriage forms the family—one of the building blocks of society—and as such provides a powerful social myth which it would be useless, perhaps even disastrous, to attempt to break. But I would favor the development of a liturgy for "holy union" for the homosexual couple, and would insist that such a holy union (perhaps "marriage" in the sight of God) needs the support of continuing relationships in the worshiping, nurturing community just as heterosexual marriages do.

Creativity, certainly in the context of man as co-creator with God, is not limited to procreation. There are many ways in which man is called upon to share creativity with God: to bring order and meaning out of personal and social chaos and to bring to fulfillment that which is only potential, to mention only two. Reuel Howe speaks in his writings of what I feel is the highest type of human creativity in this context. Howe, affirming that a person is a person only in meaningful relationship to another (the Thou-Thou relationship discussed above), says that we can "call one another into being." By being responsible, responsive, personal, and caring, we can help another to become truly a person by affirming his being.[50]

Man's deepest longings are not for sexual relationship *per se*, but for significant self-affirming and other-affirming relationships. Sexual promiscuity, both hetero- and homo-, among other drives is motivated by this universal desire to escape the loneliness and personal extinction that result when his personhood is not affirmed by others. Perhaps this is the reason Jesus was much more lenient with the sensual sinner (the adultress and the prostitute) than he was with the pious hypocrite and those who were not in responsive, affirming relationships with other people.

The Gospel proclaims that we are accepted by God, that to be "in the Kingdom" is to be both accepted and therefore accepting persons. Christ was concerned about the quality of the relationships between persons, and pointed out that relationship to God is only possible through responsible relationships with other persons. He taught us that love of God and neighbor liberates man into fullness of life—liberates us from the bondage of estrangement, anxiety, and hostility.

It is part of the mission of the Church to enable these kinds of person-affirming relationships to occur. There is no indication in Christ's teachings that the quality of life he lived and which he envisioned for all men, and which the Church is called to manifest in the world, was limited to heterosexually-oriented persons.

If the homosexual is accepted by God, a belief which is implicit in this paper, then he can be an accepting person, and this includes self-acceptance. Thielicke is provocative on this point:

> *What then does "acceptance" mean here? It can mean*
> *to accept the burden of this predisposition to homo-*
> *sexuality only as a divine dispensation and see it as a*
> *task to be wrestled with, indeed—paradoxical as it may*
> *sound—as a* talent to be invested. *(Luke 19:13f)* [51]

And when the "master of the servants" comes and settles accounts with us (Matthew 25:19, Luke 19:15), he will not ask what talent we have had (none of us asked for what we got) for he knows that already. But he will ask to see what we have done with that which has been given us.

The question of ethics, of responsible, responsive relationships, comes naturally to the fore at this point, but that goes beyond the scope of this paper. Thielicke points out:

> *We may assume that the homosexual has to realize his*
> *optimal ethical potentialities on the basis of his irrevers-*
> *ible situation.* [52]

The homosexual, no less than the heterosexual, needs understanding and sympathetic pastoral guidance in his struggle for ethical fulfillment. The homosexual, no less than the heterosexual, needs the spiritual and emotional support of a Church which enables redemptive relationships to occur. These needs are largely unfulfilled at the present time; it is crucial that we concern ourselves with them in the immediate future. The rapid emergence of the Metropolitan Community Church as a national movement of Christian Gay people can, in this context, only be seen as a judgment on the Church and on the Church's outdated and painfully inadequate understanding of this aspect of human sexuality.

NOTES

1. The Wolfenden Report, *Report of the Committee on Homosexual Offenses and Prostitution (New York: Lancer Books, 1964).*

2. Lee, Ronald, *"Gay Liberation and Mental Health,"* The National Conference on Social Welfare Proceedings, *1972 (New York: Columbia University Press, 1972).*

3. *DePuy, Norman, "God's Gays," in* American Baptist *(October 1971), p. 2. Quoted from a reprint published by the Minnesota Council for the Church and the Homophile.*

4. *Bailey, Derrick Sherwin,* Homosexuality and the Western Christian Tradition *(New York: Longmans, Green and Company, 1955), p. viii. Bailey says "the tradition [regarding homosexuality] has not undergone any significant alterations since the end of the Middle Ages."*

5. *Among recent books dealing with the subject are: H. Kimball Jones,* Toward a Christian Understanding of the Homosexual *(1966); Ralph Weltge, ed.,* The Same Sex *(1969); Henri J. M. Nouwen,* Intimacy *(1969); Troy Perry,* The Lord Is My Shepherd and He Knows I'm Gay *(1972); and W. Norman Pittenger,* Making Sexuality Human *(1970).*

6. *Bailey, op. cit., p. ix.*

7. *A good example of the assumed righteousness of society's attitude is a remark attributed to someone in the San Francisco Police Department when ministers from CRH were informing the police of the forthcoming ball (January 1, 1965): "If you aren't going to enforce God's law, we are." See "The Council on Religion and the Homosexual," by Del Martin in* Essays on Religion and the Homosexual, *vol. I (n.d.), p. 20.*

8. *Snaith, N. H., in* The Interpreter's Bible, *vol. 3 (New York: Abingdon Press, 1954), pp. 130-131.*

9. *Baab, O. J. "Prostitution," in* The Interpreter's Dictionary of the Bible, *vol. K-Q (New York: Abingdon Press, 1962), pp. 931 ff.*

10. *Bailey, op. cit., pp. 49-53.*

11. *In addition to R.S.V., see New English Bible—"male prostitute"; and Jerusalem Bible—"men . . . who were sacred prostitutes."*

12. *Bailey, op. cit., p. 3.*

13. *Bailey, p. 9.*

14. *Bailey, p. 10.*

15. *Bailey, pp. 10-26.*

16. *Bailey, p. 155.*

17. *For example, Theodore H. Gaster,* Myth, Legend and Custom in the Old Testament *(New York: Harper and Row, 1969), pp. 158-159.*

18. *Rash, John, "Reforming Pastoral Attitudes Towards Homosexuality,"* Union Seminary Quarterly Review, *vol. XXV, 4 (Summer 1970). Quotation from a report by The Minnesota Council for the Church and the Homophile, p. 5.*

19. *von Rad, Gerhard,* Genesis, A Commentary *(Philadelphia: Westminster Press, 1961), pp. 212 ff.*

20. *Laymon, Charles M., ed. (New York: Abingdon Press, 1971), p. 17.*

21. *Bailey, op. cit., pp. 59-60.*

22. *Thielicke, Helmut,* The Ethics of Sex, *trans. by John W. Doberstein (New York: Harper and Row, 1964).*

23. *Thielicke, p. 279.*

24. *Knox, John,* The Interpreter's Bible, *vol. 9 (1954), p. 401.*

25. The Interpreter's Bible, *vol. 9 (1954), p. 400.*

26. *Thielicke, op. cit., p. 282.*

27. *Bailey, op. cit., pp. 38 ff.*

28. *Marmor, Judd, ed.,* Social Inversion: The Multiple Roots of Homosexuality *(New York: Basic Books, 1965).*

29. *See Reiss, Albert J., Jr., "The Social Integration of Queers and Peers," in Hendrick M. Ruitenbeek, ed.,* The Problem of Homosexuality in Modern Society *(New York: E. P. Dutton, 1963), pp. 249f.*

30. *Marmor, op. cit., p. 4.*

31. *Marmor, p. 19.*

32. Ibid.

33. *Hooker, Evelyn, "The Adjustment of the Male Overt Homosexual,"* The Journal of Projective Techniques, *21:18-31 (1957), p. 31.*

34. *Marmor, op. cit., p. 5.*

35. *Pare, C. M. B., "Etiology of Homosexuality: Genetic and Chromosomal*

Aspects," in Marmor, pp. 77-79.

36. Marmor, op. cit., p. 16.

37. A quotation from the Hampsons' report of their studies of the acquiring of the gender role by humans, reported by Marmor, p. 9.

38. Marmor, op. cit., p. 10.

39. Hoffman, Martin, The Gay World: Male Homosexuality and the Social Creation of Evil (New York: Basic Books, 1968).

40. Marmor, op. cit., p. 16.

41. Rash, op. cit., p. 2, with credit to Hoffman, op. cit., pp. 123-129.

42. Thielicke, op. cit., pp. 3f.

43. Thielicke, p. 4.

44. Barth seems to have struggled with this issue and in later writings enlarges on the meaning. David Cairns, in The Image of God in Man (S. C. M. Press, Ltd., 1953) points out that while Barth does say that "a human being will in any case only be such before God and among his kind upon the conditions, that it is as a man in relationship to the woman, or woman in relationship to the man," he nevertheless admits that the sexual distinction between "I" and "Thou" in mankind "belongs to our nature as creatures, and not to the image." In addition, says Cairns, Barth does himself later admit that women in a nunnery can have a real personal existence, while Goethe with his ocean of mistresses failed to achieve a fully personal relation with others. He explains that the relation of man to woman of which he speaks is not in conflict to the relation between man and wife, but covers all the relations between men and women, such as that between mother and son, or father and daughter, or brother and sister. While the relationship is at its highest and most difficult and dangerous in the bond between husband and wife, and also at its most rewarding, yet the whole nexus of personal relations between one sex and the other is an example of personal relationship par excellence." (pp. 175 ff.).

     Brunner, on the other hand, while not ignoring the significance of the sexual, nevertheless stresses the fact that man can "only be human in community." Cairns says, in paraphrasing Brunner's thought: "For God does not only give himself to us in the Word; He gives us our neighbor also. With the Divine 'Thou' there is also given to us the human 'thou,' as the condition of man's existence as a self. For man cannot be man in isolation

. . . and this human 'thou' is thus not something accidental to our humanity, but it is the very condition of our being men. Thus we get a new definition of humanity, *which finds its kernel not in the creative power of freedom, nor in cognitive reason, but* in fellowship as fulfillment of responsibility" *(p. 150).*

45.   *Thielicke,* op. cit., *p. 6.*

46.   *For example, if Thielicke's statement (*ibid., *p. 283) "the status of existence which we all share as men in the disordered creation that exists since the Fall," is a historical statement, then it does not make sense, though theologians have been talking in these terms for centuries. If, on the other hand, he is speaking metaphorically of existential reality—the persistent distortion and disordering of the Creator's intent by the would-be-autonomous creature—"since the Fall" refers to every man's history and to a cumulative social fabric of sin and the results of sin into which every man is born, hence the "disordered creation which we all share as men," then the Fall can be a meaningful concept.*

47.   *Thielicke,* op. cit., *p. 283.*

48.   *See Marmor, pp. 18 ff.*

49.   *Thielicke,* op. cit., *p. 286.*

50.   *See Reuel Howe,* Man's Need and God's Action *(Greenwich, Conn.: The Seabury Press, 1957), and* Herein Is Love *(Valley Forge, Pa.: The Judson Press, 1961).*

51.   *Thielicke,* op. cit., *p. 284.*

52.   *Thielicke, p. 285.*

We are trapped by time in our efforts to keep things updated. Between the writing and the publication of this book, the Gay movement within the church will have taken many more historic steps. This chapter, which records only some of the milestones of the past few years, must be understood in terms of this reality. It does not attempt to be a comprehensive history but simply seeks to communicate a feeling for the movement in the church.—Eds.

THE GAY MOVE- MENT IN THE CHURCH

SALLY GEARHART AND BILL JOHNSON

LESBIANS AND THE MOVEMENT

In the following account of the Gay movement in the church, it is significant that Lesbians are virtually invisible. We can be absolutely certain that this is *not* because there are no Lesbians in the church; nor is it because there are no Lesbians in professional positions in denominational structures. It is rather because Lesbians as yet have chosen not to share their identity with the church.

Only the women themselves can speak about the personal pressures that keep them silent on the subject of their Lesbianism. When they choose to speak they will unquestionably be heard, particularly if they hold professional roles within the church. Meanwhile, their reasons for remaining anonymous and silent can be understood in light of the following:

1. Like the Gay man who remains silent, the Lesbian often feels she can heal more wounds and fight more effectively by masquerading as a heterosexual than she can by being open and risking almost certain disavowal. The conflict—to be open or to remain closeted—is heightened for the Lesbian because

she feels her struggle to be not just against a church that hates same-sex love but also against the whole of masculist theology. The question of where the changes can best be made—inside or outside the church—is intensified. As one woman has put it, the question is whether to stay in and be a closet dyke or get out and be a closet Christian.

2. The Lesbian has sacrificed more than men have to get where she is. Because she is a woman trying to make it in an institution that ignores and devalues her experience as a woman, she must play by men's rules. That makes it different and harder. Because she loves another or others like herself—and probably herself as well—and still identifies with an institution that can tolerate neither same-sex love nor self-esteem on the part of women, she has to hide. That makes it different again. She is twice different. And if she loses, she loses more than even her Gay brother does, since economic realities provide fewer jobs for women than for men. For open Lesbians there are fewer still.

3. The Lesbian's feminism—which may be only beginning to grow—commits her to supporting her Gay brothers in their frontal attack on ecclesiastical structures, for both she and they are challenging sex-roles and concepts of family design. But that very feminism suggests that the woman's way is different, that her action will have to be in concert with other women, heterosexual as well as Lesbian. The Gay man does not yet enjoy the solidarity with heterosexual men that the Lesbian is just beginning to find with her heterosexual sisters. This makes the Gay man's posture as lonely, often, as it is courageous; it makes the Lesbian's choice of commitment a painful one.

One of the few forums for Lesbians within a Christian context has been provided by the Metropolitan Community Church (MCC), a church whose membership is primarily Gay. MCC is in the large majority male—perhaps as much as 90 percent of its members are Gay men. However, the ministry of the Reverend Freda Smith of Sacramento's MCC may well spark Christian Lesbians into renewed church activity. Her commitment and enthusiasm have commanded respect from MCC members across the country. In the fall of 1973 she became the first woman to be elected to the Board of Elders of the Universal Fellowship of Metropolitan Community Churches.

MCC congregations are also the sponsors of Sandra Schuster and Madeleine Isaacson, two Lesbian mothers who were at one point in full flight with their six children down the California coast; close on their heels were a brace of lawyers and two puzzled and angry husbands. Finally, in an historic Seattle court decision, they were granted custody of all their children on the condition that each of them (and her children) maintains a residence separate from the other (and her children). Sandy and Madeleine's case is one of the first instances of open Lesbians' being given child custody. They believe that their Christian faith had something to do with the final granting of that custody; both of the women have been strong church members both before and throughout their relationship. MCC has made it possible for them to tell their story and to proclaim with laughter, pathos, joy, and song the presence of God at the center of their loving relationships as a family. With these notable exceptions, the Gay movement within the church has been largely a male endeavor.

GAY PEOPLE TOGETHER

In June 1969, when the Christopher Street Riots outside the Stonewall Inn in New York City gave rise to the Gay Liberation Movement, militant Gays were not thinking about relating to the institutional church. The goals of the newest liberation movement were primarily social and political; it was conceived of as a movement for basic human and civil rights. The immediate concern was to eliminate police harassment and discriminatory law enforcement. Concern also focused on the need to enable Gay women and men to come to a new and/or deeper understanding of their own personal dignity and worth. Indeed, social oppression had touched the lives of Gay people very deeply. The homophobic society had so inculcated self-hatred that there was as much consciousness raising to do within the Gay community as there was in the society at large. The amount of work to be done was staggering; yet Gay persons who openly affirmed their Gayness and gave themselves to the struggle were sustained by the knowledge that was written on their hearts—that their experience of love was true and strong. The knowledge of the beauty of Gay love, the meaning of Gay relationships, the freedom inherent in the experience of self-affirmation—these added up to the truth the movement declared: "Gay is Good."[1] The truth was often embraced with difficulty. For too long, Gay people had heard and unconsciously accepted society's oppressive labels: pervert, criminal, sinner.

In 1964 the Council on Religion and the Homosexual (CRH) began its pioneering work in recognition of the need for dialogue between the religious and Gay communities. But the majority of Gay people in 1969, activists and non-activists alike, viewed the church as hopelessly homophobic and anti-life. As evidenced at the consultation that resulted in the creation of CRH (see Chapter 1) Gay people keenly felt the oppressiveness of the church. Even liberal derominations such as the United Church of Christ, which had financially supported CRH from its inception (and continues to do so), were reticent about addressing the issues of Gay liberation in other meaningful ways. Such denominations recognized that the civil rights of Gay people were daily violated by discriminatory law enforcement, but they were content with making one-time statements deploring such practices. They initiated no meaningful action to hasten the day when such practices would end.

The apathy and/or sympathetic but inactive concern of liberal denominations was not surprising. It is abundantly clear that all liberation struggles grow out of discontent, anger, and hunger for freedom on the part of those who are oppressed. Power structures, particularly those dependent upon voluntary support, cannot realistically be expected to involve themselves in such a struggle unless they are forced to do so by circumstances or by ethical, personalized challenges. It is too much to expect the church, specifically, to act simply because it has been entrusted with the Gospel of liberation. History readily testifies to the fact that the institutionalized Body of Christ will act only under one condition: when it can no longer deny the Machiavellian role it has played in prolonging oppression.

Thus the initiative for meaningful change rested squarely on the shoulders of Gay people. As Gay consciousness has evolved, individuals have begun to understand the direct relationship between traditional Judeo-Christian attitudes and Gay oppression. The legal sanctions against the expression of Gay love are rooted in religious doctrine. Likewise, attitudes in the field of psychology embraced and endorsed by professionals are founded upon the presumption that any variation of the female/male sexual relationship is abnormal—a point of view clearly influenced by religious mythology. Traditional Judeo-Christian attitudes have resulted in the overt oppression of Gay people in the religious community: the condemnations openly hurled at Gay sisters and brothers who, in good conscience, affirm themselves as Gay to their pastors, priests and rabbis; the ostracism experienced in church and community by Lesbians and Gay brothers whose orientation becomes known; the defrocking of ministers and the abandonment by the church of countless Gay persons who are told they cannot be Gay and be included in God's love.

Our need to speak the truth forcefully to the religious community has grown increasingly evident. The work of CRH and of similar councils around the country has taken on a new importance. Gay liberation struggles must now be waged on the battlefield of the institutional church if meaningful change in the attitudes of society is to be accomplished. Our understanding has grown since 1969. Our twofold task of education and advocacy continues to be overwhelming.

ALTERNATIVES TO OPPRESSION

In 1968, a year before the Stonewall Rebellion in New York City, the Reverend Troy D. Perry, a Pentecostal minister, responded to the simple words of a Gay brother who believed he had been abandoned by God. The brother's belief had been carefully nurtured. He was but one of thousands whose human dignity had been violated by the church. Troy Perry, perhaps foolishly courageous but certain that he was being led by the Holy Spirit, set himself to the task of founding a Christian church that would welcome Gay people. The church he envisioned would give to Lesbians and Gay men the Good News historically denied them by the major religious institutions. His action was as radical as the ministry of the one whose Body the church claims to be.

In October 1968 Metropolitan Community Church of Los Angeles was founded—a church for all people with a special outreach to Gay people. It is important to realize that MCC served a purpose different from the education/advocacy purposes of organizations like CRH. CRH was founded to enable dialogue and understanding between Gay people and the established religious institutions which gave them neither welcome nor affirmation. Troy Perry, a minister, was responding to the needs of Gay people abandoned by the churches of their heritage, providing a congregation where they would be welcomed, understood and affirmed.

Since 1968, MCC has grown from one congregation in Los Angeles to more than fifty churches nationwide and several missions in other countries. The combined membership numbered 15,000 people in early 1974, evidence of the degree of alienation experienced by Gay people in mainline churches. Much of MCC's growth is the direct result of Troy Perry's dynamism. He was the first truly charismatic leader in the Gay community.

Many criticize MCC as promoting a segregation of Gay people. But it is important to recognize the absolutely essential ministry that this denomination is providing for and with Gay people—a ministry which is open to them nowhere else and which most mainline denominations have not even begun to comprehend, much less initiate. Not only does MCC serve the traditional pastoral needs of Gay people; it also has developed special ministries to Gay prisoners and disabled Gay people, particularly the deaf. The existence of the Universal Fellowship of Metropolitan Community Churches should be understood not as a segregation of Gay people but as an indictment of the segregated, noninclusive nature of the mainline denominations which have caused Gay people to feel unwelcomed.

There is room for criticism. MCC, as a denomination, is basically a patriarchal (male-dominated) church. Some people within it see the need to deal more honestly with the issues of sexism. MCC must also deal with its potential to become as disastrously noninclusive of heterosexuals as mainline churches have been toward Gay people. Nevertheless, its very existence as a Christian community of faith in which Gay people experience the freedom to be real cannot be ignored.

The painful need that MCC filled was only one of many. As the function of the church became more obvious, the inspiration behind it grew contagious. In January 1972, a group of Jewish Gay persons who had been relating to Metropolitan Community Church in Los Angeles decided to organize a synagogue for Jewish Gays. Metropolitan Community Temple (MCT) was founded in Los Angeles and has developed cordial relationships with other Jewish synagogues in Los Angeles and the Hebrew Union for the Southwest. By December 1973, a Metropolitan Community Temple had been organized in New York City and a group of Jewish Gay people in Montreal were discussing organizing a Metropolitan Community Temple in that city.

One year after Troy Perry began his historic work in Los Angeles, a Roman Catholic priest, Father Pat Nidorf, OSA, of San Diego, determined that the time had come for the Catholic church to respond realistically to the needs of Gay Catholics. No religious patriarchy is more oppressive to Gay people than the Roman Catholic Church. The strict posture Catholicism takes against Gay relationships is based on this church's absolute insistence that procreation is the only moral function of sexuality. The burden of condemnation laid upon the lives of Gay persons by the Catholic church has led in more than a few cases to suicide. The moralistic admonitions of many priests to "change or abstain" have caused countless Gay Catholics to leave the communion of the church, to denounce it, and to revile it.

Thus, in 1969, out of pastoral concern, Fr. Nidorf, with the permission of his superior, founded Dignity, an organization for Gay Catholics. Fr. Nidorf sought to bring a new word of acceptance and hope to Gay people who had denounced the church, and to Gay priests and lay persons who, for whatever reasons, had maintained a relationship to the communion.

The growth of Dignity across the country has been significant, although many Gay Catholics are reluctant even to communicate with the organization since it is associated with the oppressive Catholic church. At the time of the first Dignity national convention in September, 1973, there were Dignity chapters in twelve major cities in the United States. Personal contact is maintained with hundreds of Gay Catholics who are unable to relate to local Dignity chapters. Gay Catholics, including many priests, have found in Dignity a rallying point, a source of hope, an organization with which they can identify and through which their concerns can be addressed to the church. Articles concerning the Catholic church's response to Gay people have appeared in several Catholic journals,[2] no doubt inspired by the very existence of Dignity.

But most important, Dignity represents the first organizing effort of Gay people within a particular tradition. Although it was organized to meet basic spiritual and communal needs, Dignity will of necessity become more and more the voice of Gay liberation within the Catholic church. At the first national convention, national officers were elected and a temporary constitution adopted in anticipation of continued growth. Plans were also made to assure the ongoing publication of the *Dignity Newsletter*, one of the finest existing vehicles for dialogue concerning Gay people and religious faith.

MCC and Dignity have both sought to minister to Gay people and to address the religious establishment as to their needs and concerns. Among themselves, MCC and Dignity members (including Gay celibates) acknowledge being Gay; but apart from their life together many relate to others as presumed heterosexuals (or as presumed heterosexual celibates). For the most part, the leaders of the MCC churches have openly affirmed their Gayness. This is not as true of the leadership of most Dignity chapters, a fact that may well be a handicap whenever Dignity seeks to speak to the church.

Perhaps more than MCC, Dignity must wrestle with its inherent sexism and the fact that it reflects the very patriarchal structure it seeks to challenge. It has the potential however, effectively to speak the new truth that will cause the Catholic church to re-evaluate its historic oppressive posture concerning Gay relationships and human sexuality. This potential might well be reflected in the fact that in March 1974 the Vatican undertook an investigation of the views of Father John McNeill, S.J., who keynoted the first Dignity convention and officially silenced him, forbidding him to speak or write concerning his views on Gay people.

ADVANCE FROM WITHIN

In 1970, the Unitarian Universalist Association (UUA) General Assembly adopted a resolution on homosexuality and bisexuality which called for an end to discrimination in law enforcement, in civil service and in the armed services. Even more significantly, the UUA resolution repudiated the sickness theory of homosexuality and called upon Unitarians to make a "special effort to assist homosexuals to find employment in our midst consistent with their abilities and desires." At least theoretically, the statement paved the way for the acceptance of openly Gay persons in the ministry of the UUA.

The adoption of the 1970 UUA resolution, successfully strategized by the Reverend Jim Stoll of San Francisco, encouraged the Reverend Richard Nash of Los Angeles and Elgin Blair of Toronto to organize a UUA Gay Caucus which would speak to Unitarians from within the denomination. The Unitarian Gay Caucus emerged at the General Assembly in 1971 and since that time has been instrumental in the development of a new UUA curriculum, "About Your Sexuality," which includes the finest denominational educational materials to appear on same-sex relationships. The curriculum, designed for persons of junior-high age and older, affirms the viability of same-sex relationships as a variant form of sexual expression. The UUA Gay Caucus has also been instrumental in the production of an adult curriculum entitled "The Invisible Minority: The Homosexuals in Our Society," which includes a series of three filmstrips.

In addition to curriculum development, Gay Unitarians organized active Gay Caucus groups in Los Angeles, Memphis, Chicago, New York City and

Toronto. The Caucus also publishes a monthly newsletter. At the 1973 General Assembly, the 175 members succeeded in securing adoption of a proposal to establish an Office of Gay Concerns (OGC) at the denominational headquarters in Boston. The victory however turned out to be a partial one, since the General Assembly allocated no funds to staff the office or to make it functional. It did commit the denomination to an effort to raise funds for the office from extra-budgetary sources. While some Unitarian Gay Caucus members were discouraged and gave up on the denomination as being hopelessly homophobic, the majority remained committed to the struggle from within. They continued to work with the UUA leadership and in April 1974, the UUA Board of Trustees voted to establish the OGC within the UUA Department of Education.

Four months after the 1970 UUA General Assembly adopted its affirmative statement, the United Church of Christ (UCC) was faced with the issue of ordaining a Gay person to the Christian ministry. In the fall of 1970, Gay seminarians in the nine theological schools of the Graduate Theological Union in Berkeley organized for the purpose of mutual support and to discuss how they, as future church professionals, would relate to the oppressive attitudes of the church toward Gay people. Two United Church of Christ students at the Pacific School of Religion—Nick Benton, a graduate student, and Bill Johnson, a senior—identified with the Gay seminarians. Nick Benton, highly qualified academically, had openly affirmed his Gayness while seeking ordination in the United Church of Christ from the Golden Gate Association of the Northern California Conference UCC. The request, complicated by the candidate's militant political posture, sparked considerable debate. Ignorance and irrational fears surfaced. Opposition to the request intensified and the debate ground to a halt when Nick Benton withdrew his request as well as his membership in the UCC, declaring the denomination hopelessly sexist.

Meanwhile, Bill Johnson had openly affirmed himself as a Gay man, and declared his intention to request ordination from the same Association. Bill was highly respected and not politically militant. He had an excellent academic record and an admirable record of service to the church. He was an almost embarrassingly ideal candidate for ordination. Nevertheless, his request represented an historic challenge and the debate it inspired lasted for a year and a half. Through it all, no one questioned his qualifications, commitment, or integrity. The request was challenged solely because of his Gay sexual orientation.

Although every level of the United Church of Christ functions autonomously, the debate in the Golden Gate Association of Northern California Conference UCC spread to the national level—to the UCC Council for Church and Ministry. The Council determined that the Association, having final authority to ordain, had also the responsibility to determine the case on its own merits. At the very same hour that the national body made its decision, delegates to the Golden Gate Association's ecclesiastical council representing the thirty-one churches of the Association voted 62 to 34 to authorize Bill Johnson's ordination to the ministry. The ordination took place on June 25, 1972, a day that also marked the third anniversary of the Stonewall Rebellion and the fifteenth anniversary of the United Church of Christ.

The significance of Bill Johnson's historic ordination is not only that an affirmed Gay person was ordained but also that a sizable community of rather ordinary lay and ordained church people opened themselves to a comprehensive educational process.[3] In freedom of conscience they voted to ordain to the ministry a candidate who is openly Gay. A decision made with much soul-searching, it required an impassioned exploration and finally rejection of the mythology which the church has perpetuated concerning Gay people for thousands of years. The majority of the voting delegates affirmed that Bill's sexual orientation had no relevance whatever to his ordination as a minister. They affirmed that God calls persons of every orientation to the important work of ministry. There is no doubt that this ordination has been a source of hope to hundreds of Gay seminarians and unaffirmed Gay ministers across the country and around the world. It has given many Gay and bisexual lay persons reason to believe that the oppressive attitude of the church can be successfully challenged and changed. The importance of honesty and integrity in the ministry has been underscored. It has inspired a dialogue in the UCC that cannot be silenced and it serves as a prophecy of things to come.

While heralded internationally as a "first" in church history, the ordination did not establish a policy or even set a precedent in the United Church. Because the power to ordain lies with each autonomous association, the decision by the Golden Gate Association had no official bearing upon future requests for ordination from Gay seminarians. Nevertheless, Bill Johnson's ordination generated such discussion within the UCC that several Conferences organized task forces to study the entire spectrum of human sexuality. The UCC Council for Church and Ministry through a Committee on Human Sexuality and Ordination continued to study the matter of ordination of affirmed homosexual persons. In October 1973, the Council for Church and Ministry adopted the following position statement:

> *In the instance of considering a stated homosexual's candidacy for ordination, the issue should not be his/her homosexuality as such, but rather, the candidate's total view of human sexuality and his/her understanding of the morality of its expression.*[4]

On October 30, 1973, the Executive Council of the United Church of Christ, the denomination's highest judicatory when the biennial General Synod is not in session, commended the Council's statement to the UCC associations throughout the country which have final authority to ordain candidates for the ministry.

The ongoing debate in the UCC and the positive response Bill Johnson had received concerning his ordination led him, in December 1972, to found the United Church of Christ Gay Caucus. Inspired by the Unitarian Gay Caucus, United Church people have developed a concept of education/advocacy from within the denomination at every level. The concept is founded upon the belief that Gay people have a right to openly and fully participate in the life of the UCC.

Four persons openly identified with the Gay Caucus at the Ninth General Synod of the UCC in June 1973. By June 1974, more than 125 persons—Gay, bisexual and heterosexual—had identified with the Caucus. Organizing is taking place at all levels of the denomination now, and a monthly newsletter is being published. A national co-ordinating committee of two women and two men exists to develop national strategies. The Caucus encourages ecumenical use of the film about Bill Johnson's ordination, "A Position of Faith," which dramatically presents the issues surrounding the ordination and opens the entire topic for discussion within local churches. Caucus members are providing leadership for educational experiences within the UCC and encouraging UCC persons in influential positions, such as Dr. W. Sterling Cary, President of the National Council of Churches, to speak out in advocacy for the civil rights of Gay women and men. In May 1974, the Caucus in Northern California Conference succeeded in securing adoption by the Conference of an Overture to the 1975 General Synod of the UCC calling for:

1) response to the special needs of Gay and Bisexual
ministers, directors of religious education and other
church professionals;
2) response to problems related to employment discrimi-
nation based on sexual orientation and/or marital status
within the United Church.[5]

The importance of organizing has been recognized by Gay people in other denominations as well. In 1971, Reverend Ron Mattson of Minneapolis founded the Committee of Concern, a group of American and Canadian Friends (Quakers), which has sought to bring the truth about Gay people to Yearly Meetings of Friends, the Friends United Meeting, the Friends General Conference, and Conservative Friends. Ron Mattson was in part motivated by the 1963 Friends statement "Toward a Quaker View of Sex." That history-making document declared, "as a condition homosexuality is not more to be deplored than left-handedness. Homosexual affection can be as selfless as heterosexual affection, and therefore is not necessarily morally worse." [6]

The emergence of Gay Friends prompted several yearly meetings to adopt affirmative statements concerning Gay people; the New York, Pacific and Philadelphia Yearly Meetings were notable in this respect. The 1972 Pacific Yearly Meeting statement, one of the best such statements adopted to date, reads in part:

Now more aware of the socially inflicted suffering of
people who love others of the same sex, we affirm the
power and joy of non-exploitive, loving relationships.
As a society and as individuals we oppose arbitrary
social, economic, or legal abridgement of the right to
share this love.[7]

Pacific Yearly Meeting also authorized the creation of an ad hoc subcommittee which will publish a working paper in 1974. The efforts of Gay Friends are directed primarily at local or yearly meetings, although in August, 1973, Ron Mattson and David M. Blamires of London Yearly Meeting raised the concerns of Gay Friends at the Friends World Committee for Consultation meeting in Australia.

In May 1973, Gay people in the American Baptist Churches in the USA (ABC) held a meeting in Lincoln, Nebraska, to discuss the concerns of Gay and bisexual people. One hundred and fifty people attended and the American

Baptist Gay Caucus emerged out of this meeting. Led by Louise Rose of Pennsylvania and the Reverend Rodger Harrison of California, the Caucus is applying for recognition as an official caucus of the American Baptist Churches in the United States. Such recognition would seat a member of the Gay Caucus on the General Board of the denomination. Because their constituency is primarily conservative, ABC denominational executives have sought to deny recognition. But others, mostly related to program agencies, are working to enable dialogue between the denomination and its Gay constituency. Prior to the 1973 ABC convention at which the Gay Caucus emerged, the ABC National Ministries Alternative Life-Style Project sponsored a weekend symposium on "Homosexuality and the ABC," which was attended by forty members of the National Ministries Board and staff. It was the first such symposium ever held designed exclusively for the national leadership of a particular denomination. Still, it is abundantly clear that the education/advocacy work which the ABC Gay Caucus intends to undertake will be met with much resistance.

At present, a request for ordination in the ABC is in process which may give encouragement to the efforts of the Caucus. A highly respected graduate of the American Baptist Seminary of the West, Randle Mixon, has affirmed his Gay sexual orientation and requested ordination. His local church, Lakeshore Avenue Baptist Church in Oakland, California, has supported his request. At the time of this writing, he is awaiting an encounter with the regional Commission on Ordination.

PERSONAL COURAGE VS. ECCLESIASTICAL FEAR

While the organizing efforts of Gay people in some denominations have been increasingly successful, other efforts have fallen victim to homophobic reactions. Among the more homophobic denominations is the United Methodist Church. When two United Methodist clergypersons, Gene Leggett of Dallas and Chuck LaMont of Chicago, openly affirmed their Gayness, Methodist hierarchies succeeded in terminating the ministerial standing of both men. In both cases, the termination was sustained on "grounds" designed to disguise the basic homophobic response inspiring the Methodist hierarchy's action. An honest discussion of the ignorance and fear that existed was never enjoined.

The structure of the Methodist Church requires each Methodist bishop to appoint all ordained persons under her/his charge to a position of ministry. Clearly a bishop would encounter certain difficulties in appointing an affirmed Gay minister because of the fear and ignorance that reside in the church, but it is equally certain that such appointments would be possible were Methodist bishops more inclined to be courageous and facilitate the educating that must take place. So far, several Methodist bishops have found it more expedient to preside over defrockings. These actions have demonstrated a complete disregard for the violence done to the careers and lives of committed clergypersons who have faithfully served the church.

The unenlightened attitudes of the United Methodist Church are reflected in the "Statement of Social Principles" adopted in 1972 by the United Methodist General Conference. After stating that "sex between a man and a woman is only to be clearly affirmed in the marriage bond," the statement refers to homosexuals as "persons of sacred worth" but then goes on to declare, "we do not condone the practice of homosexuality and consider this practice incompatible with Christian doctrine."[8]

Although the Methodist National Board of Christian Social Concerns spent many months developing a basically liberal, positive statement for presentation to the 1972 General Assembly, the delegates, on a wave of homophobia, adopted the final regressive statement that was written on the floor of the Conference. Efforts by a Methodist layperson, Ernest Reaugh of Albany, New York, to organize a Methodist Gay Caucus for the 1972 General Conference never succeeded. Thus no viable education/advocacy group existed to deal with the fear reactions that emerged.

But the movement in the Methodist Church is not dead. Gay Methodists are quietly organizing in several parts of the country, particularly in California, Illinois and Texas. A layperson, Troy Stokes of San Antonio, is coordinating the organizing of Methodists, and support for the struggle of Gay women and men has been expressed by several program agencies—notably the United Methodist Council on Youth Ministry. In January 1974, that body adopted a resolution asking that homosexuality "not be a bar to the ministry." The next General Assembly of the United Methodists will be held in 1976. At that time it is expected that the Methodist condemnation of Gay people will be challenged and obliterated by the united effort of several groups within the denomination.

On another front, in the spring of 1973, United Presbyterians in Chicago acted against the Reverend David Sindt and against the Lincoln Park Presbyterian Church of Chicago. David Sindt, an openly Gay Presbyterian minister, had been called to the staff of Lincoln Park Church to develop a specialized ministry with the Gay community. The ministry proposal, developed by the Session of Lincoln Park Church, presented a basic concept of mutual ministry between the church and the Gay community and not a paternalistic ministry to the Gay community. The church was to be ministered to by Gay people through their open involvement in its life, even as the needs of the Gay community would be ministered to by the church.

According to ecclesiastical procedures, in order for David Sindt to accept the call to the staff of Lincoln Park Church, clearance for acceptance was needed from the Committee on Ministerial Relations of the Presbytery of Chicago. That committee studied the matter for a year before ruling not to recommend final clearance for David Sindt to accept the call from the Lincoln Park congregation. In its report, the Committee on Ministerial Relations stated:

> . . . it is important that the minister not be himself an advocate of homosexuality, as then homosexuality would simply be another form of idolatry. Our conversation with Mr. Sindt indicates that he was a committed advocate of homosexuality and his defensiveness of the Gay Liberation Movement would tend to lead to a ministry exclusive of heterosexuals.[9]

The Ministerial Relations Committee made its decision without consulting any openly Gay people. A three-person subcommittee of the Ministerial Relations Committee met with David Sindt for only two hours two days before the final motion was adopted. The committee totally failed to understand the mutual-ministry concept described in the proposal and, more tragically, failed to comprehend that by denying clearance to David Sindt, it was testifying to the noninclusive nature of the United Presbyterian Church. Clearly the committee members, victims of their own ignorance and probably afraid of a backlash from conservative Presbyterians as well, voted to sustain the mythology that a person cannot be Gay and Christian at the same time.

Upon receiving the ruling of the Committee on Ministerial Relations, the Session of Lincoln Park Presbyterian voted to reaffirm its proposal and to call

David Sindt as a lay person, though ordained, to work with the congregation in the development of its new ministry with the Gay community. He accepted the call and is also serving now as a field education supervisor for a Gay Methodist seminarian from McCormick Theological Seminary in Chicago. He has also been approved as a supervisor for field education by Garrett (Methodist) and Seabury-Western (Episcopal) seminaries. In the light of these enthusiastic acknowledgements of David Sindt's credibility as a minister and educator, the prejudice of the Committee on Ministerial Relations becomes even more evident.

In November 1973, David Sindt began the work of organizing a Gay Caucus among Presbyterians. Members of the Presbyterian Gay Caucus attended the United Presbyterian General Assembly in June 1974 to advocate a change in the denomination's essentially negative posture toward Gay women and men.

In 1972 in an Episcopal diocese an affirmed Gay seminarian encountered difficulty when he requested standing as a postulant, the first stage of progression toward ordination to the Episcopal priesthood. According to the seminarian, the diocesan Commission on Ministry was predisposed to reject the request for postulancy of any affirmed Gay person, although it is widely assumed in the Gay community that there is a high proportion of closeted Gay men in the Episcopal priesthood. During the months of debate, the seminarian reported that he was required to undergo excessive psychological testing and was pressured to drop his request so as not to create a controversy in the diocese. Finally, the seminarian was granted standing as a postulant. However, when the period of postulancy was completed, he was informed that he would not be admitted to candidacy for ordination.

It is probable that the seminarian would have been admitted to candidacy had he participated in a conspiracy of silence concerning his Gayness. As in most denominations, it is more acceptable to be Gay in the Episcopal seminary and priesthood as long as one does not openly identify oneself as such —that is, relate to the church with honesty. The propensity of Gay men to remain closeted seems especially acute within the patriarchal Episcopal church. An Episcopal layperson, John Preston, founder of the Minnesota Council for the Church and the Homophile, has had limited success at organizing Gay Episcopalians. As of this writing, the Episcopal church has not ordained women to the priesthood and indeed, at its October 1973 conference in

Louisville, Kentucky, some delegates were heard who opposed the ordination of women on the grounds that since the church is female, such ordination would constitute a "Lesbianization of the church." Nevertheless, it is certain that affirmed Gay persons and feminists will continue to challenge the Episcopal patriarchy and confront the hypocrisy of the type encountered by the Gay seminarian and by Episcopal women.

The actions against Gene Leggett, Chuck LaMont, David Sindt, and the Episcopal seminarian are indicative of the historical and hysterical response of the church to Gay people. These persons are not alone. Countless other church professionals have been made victims of scandal, defrocked, prematurely retired, or abandoned by actions grounded in ecclesiastical fear. Gay seminarians have been pressured into forsaking their call to the ministry by administrators and denominational executives who were fearful of truth and unable to cope with reality—perhaps even the reality of their own lives. It is impossible to calculate the number of lives that have been violated or destroyed, the number of careers ruined, but surely thousands have been victims. Thousands more maintain their positions in the church by carefully guarding the secret of their identity. Intimidated into silence and self-repression by the church's injustice and discrimination, they live with the constant fear of exposure.

FROM CONFRONTATION TO DIALOGUE

The movement within the church is increasingly gaining strength in demanding an intensified dialogue between the Gay and religious communities. Organizations such as the Council on Religion and the Homosexual are constantly being called upon for resources and guidance. Reluctantly, denominations are beginning to take seriously the fact that Gay people *within* the church will no longer silently accept oppression. Gay seminarians have organized in the four major theological centers in the United States—Berkeley, Boston, Chicago, and New York. Members of the Gay Caucus at Union Theological

Seminary in New York City have joined with other students in calling for the creation of a "Theological Center on Human Sexuality," which would explore issues of human sexuality as they relate to church doctrine and tradition and begin the re-education process that must follow such exploration. Gay seminarians in schools in New Haven, Atlanta, St. Louis, Kansas City, Rochester, and Claremont, California, and other cities are identifying with each other for mutual support. Gay caucuses are also being organized among the Disciples of Christ, the Lutheran Church in America, the American Lutheran Church and Missouri Synod Lutherans. The concerns of Gay and bisexual people will increasingly be presented to denominational meetings and program agencies.

Articles about Gay consciousness, Gay people, and the response-ability of the church have appeared in a number of major religious publications. In Winter 1972 the final issues of *Motive*, an excellent Methodist publication, were devoted to Lesbian/feminism and Gay men. These issues were published independently by *Motive's* Gay staff members after the Methodist Church decided to cease publication of the magazine. The reason for that decision was rumored to be historically rooted in the appearance of the March/April 1969 issue which strongly advocated women's liberation.

Still another controversy surrounded the July/August 1973 issue of *Trends*, a United Presbyterian publication. That issue, entitled "Homosexuality: Neither Sin nor Sickness," presented a thesis concerning the health and wholeness of Gay people that was in conflict with the United Presbyterian denominational position. In 1970, the 182nd General Assembly of the United Presbyterian Church, USA, had added an appendix to a reasonably positive position paper by the Council on Church and Society that declared adherence to the belief that " . . . the practice of homosexuality is sin."[10] But Florence Bryant and Dennis Shoemaker, the editors of *Trends*, held fast and produced the finest publication to date by a major denomination on the issue of Gay people and the church. Preparing the issue for publication sparked another controversy. An article by Sally Gearhart on Lesbian feminism, "The Lesbian and God the Father, or All the Church Needs is a Good Lay—on Its Side," was censored from the issue by United Presbyterian Program executive Robert Kempes. Following publication of the censored issue, Florence Bryant resigned in protest. *Trends* came under attack from conservative Presbyterians who, being basically ignorant of the truth which *Trends* explored comprehensively, have relentlessly expressed their anger that such an issue was even published. They called for the firing of Dennis Shoemaker, who subsequently resigned. In April, 1974, the Presbyterians announced *Trends* would cease publication.

Articles concerning Gayness have appeared in the *Christian Century, U.S. Catholic, Commonweal, Christianity and Crises,* and *Engage/Social Action.* The appearance of such articles indicates a growing awareness on the part of the church that it can no longer avoid the concerns and the needs of Gay people. The resulting dialogue concerning religion and Gay consciousness has prompted other publications, notably *Awake* and *Christianity Today,* to publish condemnatory articles reiterating and upholding the mythology and biblical admonitions traditionally used to justify prejudice against Gay people. Such condemnations are clearly based upon a selective use of the scriptures. Passages are quoted out of context, and the articles simply lack responsible biblical scholarship. Unfortunately, the effect of such articles is not limited to those communities which depend upon blind allegiance to biblical literalism. Often, persons who are otherwise theologically liberal use such biblical literalism to justify their prejudice against homosexuality and Gay people, masking their homophobia in a "condemnation by God"—that is, a condemnation entirely innocent of the intelligent, scholarly use of biblical record. Nevertheless, liberal denominations are increasingly seeking to respond to the concerns of Gay people in the church.

Apart from the personal confrontations discussed earlier, denominational bodies have responded primarily in two ways: by making statements or initiating action on the local level. Though there is little real practical value in statement-making, there is value in the dialogue that takes place as a statement or resolution is being developed and debated. Most denominational statements to date have focused upon the reasonably noncontroversial matter of discriminatory law enforcement. As early as 1969, a fine resolution by the United Church of Christ Council for Christian Social Action (CCSA) stated:

> *The Council for Christian Social Action hereby declares*
> *its opposition to all laws which make private homosexual*
> *relations between consenting adults a crime and thus*
> *urges their repeal. The CCSA also expresses its opposition*
> *to the total exclusion of homosexuals from public employ-*
> *ment and from enlistment and induction into the Armed*
> *Forces, especially the dismissal by less than honorary dis-*
> *charges from the Armed Forces for homosexual practices*

> *with consenting adults in private . . .*
>
> *The CCSA also opposes, where they exist, police*
> *practices of entrapment and enticement in their attempts*
> *to enforce laws against homosexual practices and solici-*
> *tation.*[11]

The resolution also called for "honest and open discussion of the nature of homosexuality in our society." The CCSA resolution, primarily the work of Dr. Lewis Maddocks, addresses the major concerns of Gay people and the law. However, it avoids the crucial matter of committing church resources to supporting efforts for sexual law reform or court challenges to the laws which are used discriminatingly against Gay people. (It should be noted here that these laws prohibit sexual acts common to heterosexual and homosexual couples alike.) It is almost exclusively the Gay man, however, who is arrested and prosecuted. (See Guy Strait's remarks in Donald Kuhn's article, Chapter 1.) The CCSA resolution has never been presented to the major judicatories of the United Church for affirmation nor has any action been initiated to give practical substance to the CCSA positions.

Another statement with the same basic intent was adopted in 1971 by the Council of the Episcopal Diocese of New York. It stated:

> *. . . while adultery, fornication, homosexual acts, and*
> *certain deviant sexual practices among competent and*
> *consenting adults may violate Judeo-Christian standards*
> *of moral conduct, we think that the Penal law is not*
> *the instrument for the control of such practices when*
> *privately engaged in, where only adults are involved, and*
> *where there is no coercion. We favor repeal of those*
> *statutes that make such practices among competent and*
> *consenting adults criminal acts.*[12]

This statement is typical of the condemnation-first-justice-second approach which most denominations take when making statements concerning Gay people. The "Judeo-Christian standards of moral conduct" make up the foundation of the very laws being denounced. Some have even been called "sodomy" laws on the false assumption that the sin of Sodom was homosexuality. There has been little evidence that any denomination has seriously—with a genuine concern for justice—delved into the life-destructive effects on Gay people of the traditional attitudes of the church and their direct relationship with the law. A Gay person who becomes a victim of the law is in fact a victim of the church as well. There will not be a significant change in the law and the discriminatory enforcement of the law until the church reconsiders its oppressive attitudes toward Gayness and Gay people and begins to use its influence to affect a change in the laws it has so undeniably helped to produce.

Statements which purport to support the concerns and rights of Gay people while perpetuating the mythology that homosexuality is intrinsically sinful are invalid. In the past, such statements have been made with little or no dialogue with Gay people themselves. Fortunately, denominational leaders are beginning to comprehend the need for a continuing dialogue not *about* but *with* Gay people. Hopefully, not only philosophical but action-oriented denominational statements will emerge out of this dialogue.

Such a trend is starting to show itself. Moved to action by a demonstration at the 1970 Diocesan Convention, the Episcopal Diocese of Michigan began to actively seek dialogue with Gay people. In late 1973, the Report of the Diocesan Commission on Homosexuality was made public. It was an excellent report. Declaring belief that "the Church is that agency in history called upon to bear witness to the all embracing love of God" and proclaiming "we have no evidence that this love does not include homosexuals," the Commission set forth the following recommendations as "the minimum price of giving substance to that mission to which the Church is committed":

> *1. The Church should take steps to create an atmosphere*
> *of openness and understanding about human sexuality*
> *and particularly about homosexuality. Programs to*
> *assist in this process should be encouraged at all levels:*
> *national, diocesan, convocational, and parochial. Such*
> *programs should be at the disposal of institutions of*
> *learning and in particular our seminaries and church-*
> *related schools.*
> *2. All ministries and professions should be open to other-*
> *wise qualified people whatever their sexual orientation.*
> *The use that any person makes of sexuality should be*
> *open to a reasonable evaluation by individuals competent*
> *to judge the relevance of such use to the exercise of the*

*ministry or other profession in question. An oppressive
or destructive use of sexuality within personal relationships, whatever the sexual preference or orientation,
should give reason to doubt the candidate's fitness for
office.*

*3. All aspects of the Church's life—education, liturgy,
pastoral care, fellowship—should be available to all
persons, and not contingent upon those persons' guaranteed heterosexuality. Gatherings for homosexuals on
church property should be accepted to the extent that
they serve the same purpose as other social gatherings
—enabling people to meet in an atmosphere of love and
acceptance.*

*4. The Church's concern for individuals and a just social
order should lead it to speak publicly for repeal of all
laws which make criminal offenses of private, voluntary
sex acts between mature persons. The Church ought also
to oppose police harassment of homosexuals and in-
vestigatory practices which sometimes verge upon entrapment. Likewise the Church should speak publicly on
behalf of homosexual persons in the area of civil rights
legislation. There should be no discrimination against
any person in housing, employment, business services
or public accommodations on the grounds of sexual
orientation.* [13]

Clearly, members of the Commission became free from their homophobia in
the encounter with Gay persons and were able to produce a statement that
reflects truth concerning Gayness and Gay people and evidences moral and
prophetic leadership.

On local levels several church bodies have made important contributions
to the ongoing struggle to bring the concerns of Gay people to the consciousness of the Community of Faith. In Minneapolis the Lesbian Resource Center
received grants of $2500 and $1800 from the Presbyterian Women in Leadership Project and the United Methodist Voluntary Services in 1973. The Methodist agency had previously given $1800 to the Gay Community Services in

Minneapolis. The United Church of Christ financially supports the Council on Religion and the Homosexual. Glide Memorial United Methodist Church in San Francisco has sought for many years to minister to the needs of Gay people. It was at Glide Church that the Reverend Lloyd Wake officiated at the first covenant service for same-sex couples ever solemnized in the United States within a congregation of a mainline denomination. Local congregations across the country have made meeting space available to a wide variety of Gay organizations. Metropolitan Community Church congregations have found a variety of local churches, ranging from Roman Catholic to Seventh Day Adventist, willing to provide meeting space for their worship services. In most cases the MCC congregation maintains a separate identity and relates to the host congregation to a minimal degree, though many persons in MCC and in mainline churches are beginning to understand the importance and the joy of interaction.

Notable among the denominations for its efforts on the local level is the American Lutheran Church. Concentrating on the need for education, the ALC has developed a three day symposium called "Matrix" which provides clergy and laity an opportunity to explore a variety of alternative life styles, among which are Gay life styles. The "Matrix" experience has enabled significant changes in attitude of nearly three thousand ALC clergy and laity since 1970. Those changed attitudes have resulted in a greater openness to Gay people and advocacy for Gay concerns on local levels.

With the exception of the ongoing educational efforts of the ALC, progress on local levels and the commitments of denominational monies to specific purposes must be viewed with cautious hopefulness. Too often these "liberal" actions are used as a rationale for noninvolvement when it becomes clear that Gay people want more than token actions of good will. Patronizing, paternalistic tokenism has been revealed more than once when Gay people, responding to a seeming openness, have associated freely in the presence of non-Gay church people—sharing the small gestures of affection or love so acceptable, so encouraged among heterosexual people. The essential meaning of the negative response can be easily summarized: "We don't mind if you are Gay. We want to help you in your struggle for liberation. But please don't do anything in our presence that will verify the fact that you are Gay—it's embarrassing." In one instance the sight of a Gay couple holding hands caused a "supportive" congregation to deny future use of its building to a Gay organization.

In March 1973 a meeting of the Governing Board of the National Council of Churches in Pittsburgh was disrupted by Gay Activists expressing their anger at the oppressive attitudes and apathy of the church. A few members of the Governing Board attempted to respond to the concerns being expressed, but it was difficult since none of the protesters identified with the church as members and were unable to express the priorities of Gay people within the church. Recognizing the need for dialogue, sympathetic members of the Governing Board facilitated a consultation on "The Church and the Gay Community." That consultation was held in September 1973 at St. Paul School of Theology, Kansas City, Missouri. Thirty persons active in eight major denominations and the Metropolitan Community Church participated.

This was the second ecumenical conference ever held: the first one, in March 1971, in New York City, failed in its purpose of engaging denominational executives in dialogue since few attended. But the participants in Kansas City came together to develop a relevant, practical proposal to which the National Council of Churches Governing Board could respond. After two days of study and consultation, a seven member National Task Force on Gay People in the Church was formed; though two of the persons, both Lesbians, are guarding their identity because of their sensitive positions within denominational structures. The five publicly identified Task Force members are:

Reverend Roy Birchard, United Church of Christ minister, and the pastor of the Metropolitan Community Church in New York City.

Reverend Rodger Harrison, American Baptist minister, pastor of the Metropolitan Community Church in Costa Mesa, California, and secretary of the American Baptist Gay Caucus.

Reverend Bill Johnson, United Church of Christ minister, Executive Director of the Council on Religion and the Homosexual, San Francisco, and co-ordinator of the UCC Gay Caucus.

John Preston, Episcopal layperson, former Director of the Minnesota Council for the Church and the Homophile, and co-ordinator of the Episcopal Gay Caucus.

Louise Rose, American Baptist layperson, president of the American Baptist Gay Caucus, and minister of music for Central Baptist Church, Wayne, Pennsylvania.

The Task Force's first goal was the creation of an official relationship with the National Council of Churches Governing Board. This was deemed important in order to provide continuous information and input to the decision-making processes of the National Council and its member communions. The Task Force decided to seek a consortia relationship with the National Council. As a consortia, the National Task Force on Gay People in the Church would have been an independent body, officially related to the National Council. The Task Force would have been responsible for its own funding but would have had the opportunity to identify itself with the Council and respond to the Council's need for resources and education as well as those of the Council's member communions.

At the Governing Board of the National Council of Churches (NCC) meeting in New York City in October 1973, the Task Force proposed to develop a national resource center for materials related to the issues of Gay liberation and the church. It also proposed sponsoring regional workshops on Gay people in the church—workshops designed to facilitate study of theological, psychological and sociological concerns—and to enable personal interaction between participants and members of the Gay community. In addition, it proposed facilitating locally initiated conferences of church people, and at least twice a year bringing together Gay people from the various denominations for the purpose of developing mutual support and cooperative strategies. The primary objective of the proposal was dialogue, not confrontation.

The proposal was considered by the Systematic Change In Society section of the Governing Board. After debating the implications and consequences of creating a consortia relationship, the section decided instead to propose the following:

> *Recommendation: The Governing Board recommends to the Division of Education and Ministry, and Church and Society that they enter into dialogue with the "Task Force on Gay People in the Church," requesting that a representative Joint Committee on Dialogue with the Task Force on Gay People in the Church, named by the two Divisions, be established prior to conversations in order to develop the procedures for dialogue, with a progress report to be reviewed by Section III in the February, 1974 meeting of the Governing Board.*[14]

On the floor of the Governing Board, an Orthodox member of the Board stated, "In light of the fact that these people live contrary to the Holy Scriptures, I move that this item be stricken from the agenda." The motion was seconded. Debate ensued in which several people declared that the National Council would never be able to justify refusing to enter into dialogue. Explanation of the proposal revealed it to be a minimal commitment on the part of the National Council and the motion to strike the proposal from the agenda was defeated. The proposal was adopted on a strong voice vote.

The significance of this action is two-fold. For the first time, the National Council of Churches openly acknowledged that there are Gay people in the church. Secondly, the National Task Force on Gay People in the Church won legitimacy as an officially recognized group that will be specifically relating to the National Council. National Council personnel were slow in appointing the joint committee with which the Task Force was to relate, but at the February 1974 Governing Board meeting in Los Angeles the Task Force continued to pursue its objectives in good faith. Disappointment and frustration concerning the foot-dragging of the National Council were firmly expressed by Task Force members. The first meeting between the Task Force and the joint committee was set for April 5, 1974.

At that meeting, members of the Task Force and the NCC Joint Committee discussed ways to bring the concerns of Gay people in the church to the Governing Board at its October 1974 meeting. Significant action, however, probably will not take place before February or October 1975. Members of the Task Force have decided to work directly with denominations while continuing to work with the National Council. The Task Force has received financial support totaling six thousand dollars from a variety of denominational agencies and the Third World Fund of the Glide Urban Center of San Francisco.

Recognizing the need to facilitate communication among the various organizing efforts within the religious community, the Board of Directors of the Council on Religion and the Homosexual has offered the services of CRH to various Gay Caucuses and to Dignity/National. Organizing efforts are now underway in thirteen mainline denominations. Complete files on the ongoing movement are maintained in the CRH office as is an up-to-date library of publications and articles related to religion and Gay sexuality and life styles. Organizing information for theological communities is also available from CRH.

Since 1964 when CRH was founded, but especially since 1969 when the

Stonewall Rebellion gave birth to the Gay Liberation Movement, the prejudicial attitudes of many in the institutional church have been changed. It has
been a slow but steady process. In spite of resistance in every denomination,
there is a growing awareness in the church that the issues of Gay Liberation
must be embraced. Deception, secrecy and hiding related to Gayness produce
pain: The church has a healing responsibility. Discrimination against Gay people and the violation of our human and civil rights are naked injustices: The
church has a responsibility to usher in the day of justice. Masking prejudice
with biblical arguments can no longer be tolerated. Through ignorance, belief in mythology, and fear of homosexuality, a community of persons who
experience love in a way different than the majority continue to be sinned
against. The church has a responsibility to join in declaring the truth that will
ultimately redeem all people to be more fully affirmative of the broad spectrum of human sexuality and thus more fully human, more fully free, and
more fully able to respond to God's love within them.

NOTES

1. *"Gay is Good" became a self-affirming phrase used widely by Gay persons in the years immediately following the Stonewall Rebellion of
1969. It was coined by Dr. Franklin Kameny, a long-time Gay activist
in Washington, D.C.*

2. *A notable example is Fehren, Father Henry, "A Christian Response to
Homosexuals," U.S. Catholic, 37 (September 1972), 6-11.*

3. *"Learning From Experience: The Ordination of an Affirmed Homosexual Person," Northern California Conference UCC, 1973.*

4. *Position statement adopted October 1973 by the Council for Church
and Ministry of the United Church of Christ.*

5. *Overture to the Tenth General Synod of the United Church of Christ by
the Northern California Conference UCC. Adopted May 18, 1974.*

6. *Heron, Alister, ed., "Toward a Quaker View of Sex," rev. ed. (London:
Friends Home Service, 1964).*

7. *Religious Society of Friends, Pacific Yearly Meeting minute adopted 17
Eighth month, 1972.*

8. *Statement of Social Principles, United Methodist Church, adopted by
General Conference, Atlanta, Georgia, 1972.*

9. Letter dated March 12, 1973 to Session of Lincoln Park Presbyterian Church, Chicago, from Robert I. Christ, Secretary, Committee on Ministerial Relations, Presbytery of Chicago, UPUSA.

10. Appendix to the Report of the Council on Church and Society, United Presbyterian Church USA: "Sexuality and the Human Community." Adopted by a vote of 356 to 347 by the 182nd General Assembly, 1970.

11. Resolution adopted by the Council for Christian Social Action, United Church of Christ, April 12, 1969.

12. Adopted by the Council of the Episcopal Diocese of New York, March 18, 1971.

13. Report of the Diocesan Commission on Homosexuality, Diocese of Michigan, Episcopal, May, 1973.

14. "Systematic Change in Society" (Section III), Report to the Governing Board of the National Council of Churches, October 12-15, 1973, agenda item XVII, proposal 6.

*I speak here as a Christian, as a minister,
and as a Gay person. I speak from within
the church, as one who identifies with
it freely and deeply, according to my faith.
Because of my love, I am compelled to
criticize the church harshly, even at the risk
of falling victim to the homophobia that
I am literally seeking to educate to death.
My awareness of the pain of my Gay
sisters and brothers within the church—
and of my own pain—requires that I speak
these truths. Hopefully I do so
affirmatively, forthrightly, and with
love, for I deeply believe that through
the truths of Gay liberation, the church
will grow to a deeper understanding of the life of the Christ.
While these words
are addressed with special emphasis to Gay
men within the church, I hope they will
resonate in the hearts and minds of all
persons, of whatever sexual orientation, who
long to be free as human-sexuals. The
insights gained from the experience of Gay
people are applicable to the lives of all
persons. Therefore to embrace these truths is
to embrace one's own possibilities.
—B. J.*

THE GOOD NEWS OF GAY LIBER- ATION

BILL JOHNSON

There comes a time in the collective life of every oppressed minority when passive acceptance of injustice is no longer possible. The moment comes and is made known not in a groundswell of rebellion but in the personal, risk-taking declarations of individuals who in word and action say "No More!" When discrimination, injustice, and the violation of dignity become intolerable, the human spirit swells with self-affirmation and revolts. Paul Tillich called the "courage to be" the ethical act in which a person affirms her/his own being in spite of those elements of her/his existence which conflict with her/his essential self-affirmation. The truly moral and ethical posture for persons under the yoke of oppression is a stance taken personally and collectively against that oppression. Such was the posture of those who stood in self-affirmation at the Stonewall Inn on Christopher Street in 1969. Such has been the posture of many others since that time.

Gay women and men are saying a resounding "No More!" to the indignities of injustice. We are saying it to the psychiatric profession for propagating the arrested theory that Gay people are sick; to the political community for sanctioning the violation of the civil rights of Gay people and for criminalizing the expression of our love; and to law enforcement agencies for their use of illegal tactics in seeking to defend a perverted public morality. But most of all, we who are Gay are declaring "No More!" to the church.

CHALLENGING THE PATRIARCHY

These words are not new to the church. For generations Gay people have been declaring an unheeded "No More!" with their feet by walking away from the church because its traditional posture and limited view of human relationships have inherently excluded persons who have the ability to experience same-sex love. Gay people have walked away because they found it impossible to reconcile the truth of who they are and the validity of their feelings with a religious faith that staunchly remains ignorant and fearful of human sexuality.

The church is a heterosexually-oriented community; it has a vested interest in the preservation of religion as a family affair. Its marriage/family orientation is firmly rooted in the Judeo-Christian heritage. As long as the church is able to perpetuate the belief that marriage and the family are the highest forms of human relationship it will be able to perpetuate itself as a heterosexual family-oriented institution. But today even many heterosexuals are questioning the traditional views of marriage, family and sexuality, recognizing that the bases for many of these views (property and economic considerations, short life expectancy, and absence of contraception) no longer exist.

The entire structure of the church is family/heterosexually oriented—from church school to youth groups to couples' groups to senior citizens organizations. Consider the number of adults who become church members "because of the kids." Personal worth is measured with strict regard to marriage and child rearing. One need only to talk briefly to a church-related, unmarried adult—Gay or not Gay—to get an idea of the deep resentment inspired by the marriage/family orientation of the church. Or consider the many times a young, unwed minister has been rejected by a pastoral search committee because she/he did not have a family. Speaking accurately, the pastoral search committee was looking for a "family man," certainly not a "family woman." Apart from the practical fact that most congregations still want two for the price of one when they call a new minister, this obsession with family status is symptomatic of a strong prejudice against unmarried persons in the church.

While there is a place in the human community for families, it is increasingly clear that the patriarchal family structure and the socialization process that occurs within it must be seriously examined and probably radically changed. Such an investigation will not be encouraged or welcomed by the church. Of all the institutions in the world, the church is the most patriarchal in essence. This essence is expressed in its theology, in its paternalistic concepts of ministry, and in its degradation of women (which, try as it may, it seems unable to relinquish). The church supports the belief, lip service notwithstanding, that men are rightfully the protectors and preservers of religious truth. Part of the preserved "truth" is the concept of God-ordained patriarchal order in male/female sexual relationships, such relationships being morally consummated only within the confines of heterosexual marriage. The very existence of same-sex relationships calls such religious mythology into question. Threatened by the truth, the patriarchal church has traditionally ignored the validity of same-sex relationships, clung to its mythology, and acted as though sexual orientation and expression were the sole measure of human worth. The message is declared in no uncertain terms: To be whole, healthy and loved of God, one *must* be heterosexual. This Bad News has been declared by the church to Gay women and men for generations.

So, with good reason, Gay people have walked out of churches. But today Gay men are saying "No More!" in another way. We are, in growing numbers, taking the step of faith and vulnerability *within* the church. By affirming our selves as whole, integrated persons, we are challenging the church to respond to us—as persons, as Christians, as Gay men—and many of our Gay sisters are making a similar challenge. We are tired of the church (and our families and society) pretending that we do not exist, hoping that by ignoring reality, tranquility will be preserved. We know that to ignore reality is to express fear. We insist that the people of the church confront their fears— many of which will disappear as they encounter the truth of who we are and learn from us of our experience of love.

GAY MEN AND THE PATRIARCHY

It is important that the church be challenged by Gay men within it since it is in fact a male controlled institution. The patriarchal system and the uses and abuses of power are things which men in our society have been especially conditioned to understand. From earliest childhood men learn the importance of dominance and control. We learn it as we learn society's definition of maleness. We learn that competition and aggression are desirable male attributes. And when one has aggressed and "won" in the competition of human interaction, dominance and control become valued. Awareness of the necessity to dominate and control that which or whomever has been "defeated" or "won over" is ingrained in male children through the socialization process. These expressions of power are central to the "understanding" most males have of themselves; and the terrifying weight of social worth and self-esteem is very much measured by them.

Dominance and control are well understood by Gay men since we have, of necessity, become liberated from such styles of relating. When two Gay men relate to one another, our competition/aggression/dominance/control indoctrination is immediately encountered. Since both men bring to the relationship the same socialized mentality, conflict is inevitable. Though competitive spirit and social aggressiveness might well have brought the two together, dominance and control are not viable styles of relating between two men who more often than not consider themselves to be equals. The conflict is sometimes resolved by mutual consent: a style of relating is achieved in which one of the men assumes a submissive, passive role while the other manifests his dominance and control. Such role-playing may or may not extend to sexual relating. This kind of resolution was once very common because Gay male couples had only the dominance/submission heterosexual relationship as a model. But it is much less common today. With a growing understanding of Gay relationships and human interaction in general, dominance and control are discarded in favor of mutuality and equality.

These insights lead naturally to a serious conclusion. Heterosexual relationships and marriage as traditionally experienced are basically unhealthy. They are based on inequality resulting from the male dominance/control mentality. That mentality extends beyond the family into the very fabric of the church. Because Gay men have come to these conclusions through very personal, soul-searching self-examinations, we are particularly sensitive to the uses/abuses of power in the patriarchal church. Our challenge is grounded in perfect certainty that our insights are true. (And it is not incidental that feminists are declaring these same truths to the patriarchal church.)

The theology and doctrines that have traditionally been used to condemn Gay men and our Gay sisters have been created and perpetuated by men. It is not only right but essential that *men* challenge such perverse theology and oppressive doctrines. Difficult as it may be for some liberal ecclesiastics to acknowledge the fact, the institutional church still gives far greater credence to men (who, of course, possess the intellect necessary for theology) than women, and generally assumes its theologians to be heterosexual men, whether they are or not. The demand by Gay people for social justice must be accompanied by an equally articulate demand for theological justice. Gay men have a special responsibility to pursue the latter with diligence.

As Treese noted in Chapter 2, from the time of Thomas Aquinas until the publishing in 1955 of *Homosexuality and the Western Christian Tradition* by D. S. Bailey, the position of the church with regard to homosexuality remained unexamined. That was a period of seven centuries. Today Bailey's book is out of print. The work of Treese and the writings of the eminent Anglican theologian W. Norman Pittenger, whose work basically affirms Gay people, have been widely ignored. Bailey, Treese and Pittenger are well-respected theologians, but the church has chosen to ignore the visceral truths declared in their writings. The church is reluctant to examine the data that would necessarily destroy the mythology upon which its prejudicial attitudes have been built. It wallows in its homophobia.

The silence of most well-respected, contemporary theologians is painful to Gay people. Failure to explore the theological presumptions being challenged by Gay people is at best irresponsible. The argument that such an investigation is not a priority is simply not acceptable. In our time, all humanity is hungering for a deeper understanding of sexuality in all its orientations and expressions. Moral integrity demands that the church re-examine its oppressive theology concerning Gayness and Gay people. We who are Gay are certain of what the outcome of that re-examination would be. We know that theology is not valid if it is simply the result of intellectualizing. It must be grounded in experience. We who are Gay know the validity of our experience, particularly the experience of our love. That love is full of meaning and is a great source of joy; it calls us out of our selves and enables us to respond to the other. Through our experience of love we experience the presence of God in our lives.

Unfortunately, the church has traditionally and primarily concerned itself with intellectual theology, showing only a secondary concern for experiential validation (to assure *some* degree of relevance). The theologizing in which Gay people within the church have engaged, grounded as it is in experience and informed by faith, must be increasingly articulated. Scholarship like that by Bailey and Treese is essential since the liberal church values scholarship. But scholarship alone does not produce a valid theology. The experience of Gay women and men must illuminate the scholarship. A contemporary theology of sexuality must be informed by contemporary realities, not the cultural realities of nineteen centuries past. I cannot overstate the importance of Gay people, especially Gay men, asking *out loud* the relevant, poignant theological questions. Our experience makes it possible for us to frame the difficult questions which will call into being a life-affirming, all-inclusive theology of sexuality that is more concerned with love than with genital interaction.

Another important reason Gay men must accept responsibility to challenge the church relates to the matter of privilege. From any perspective, men in our society and in the church particularly are in a privileged position. Even Gay men who are "theologically condemned" are privileged in relation to women. Ordained women, even in the United Church of Christ which in its heritage has been ordaining women since the nineteenth century, have tremendous difficulty obtaining positions at equal pay within the church. Decision-making bodies at every level, though supposedly influenced by input from women, youth, Blacks, Native Americans, and Third World people, are still for the most part male controlled.

If the church is ever to become meaningfully responsive to the concerns and needs of Gay people, Gay men must be willing to become vulnerable, even though we jeopardize and in all probability lose our positions of privilege by speaking out. Those who have a genuine commitment to truth and justice—a commitment sadly absent in the lives of far too many men, Gay and not Gay, in the church—will be strong enough to take the risk. But men in our society can never fully lose their male privilege, so ingrained is it in the social structure. It is easier for an affirmed Gay male than for an affirmed Lesbian to make a living inside and outside the church. Accepting the responsibility for enlightening the church may lose us some privileges, but we will not starve.

Still, it is not easy for Gay men to declare "No More!" to the church. It means standing in opposition to an unexamined tradition that is the source of

every form of discrimination we suffer. It means opposing the patriarchal structure that as men we are not only expected to support but also to defend. It means
opening ourselves to *self*-criticism so that we can understand the ways in which
we as church-related men have contributed to the continuing oppression of our
sisters, Lesbians as well as heterosexual and bisexual women.

The resistance we meet takes subtle forms. Many men in the church, lay and
ordained alike, find our openness as affirmed Gay men threatening, in part because of their own desire to be free from the heterosexual male role/mentality/
expectation, and their subtle fear of persons who have attained such freedom.
Some are in conflict because our openness unavoidably reminds them of their
own Gay feelings which, bowing to the "authority" of the church and a homophobic society, they have carefully repressed. Our affirmation of same-sex feelings between men challenges society's disapproval of all forms of male intimacy
—emotional, intellectual, physical and spiritual. Our affirmation declares that it
is good for men to touch one another's bodies and one another's lives and that
such touching may or may not be extended to sexual relationship. Still other
men in the church find the openness of Gay men threatening because it is perceived as an affirmation of those qualities considered "feminine"—emotion, sensitivity and co-operativeness—and a denial of the usefulness of competition. And
inherent in the need to denounce Gay men is the cancer of woman-hatred. Gay
men are living reminders that the stud/macho image of the male is unhealthy,
that calling conquest and procreation "virility" and 'domination'and control
"strength," is a disease.

Openly Gay men must endure certain frustrations. Our multidimensional lives
become overshadowed by the demands upon us as spokespersons for our thousands of closeted Gay brothers. And we encounter dozens of people who, as an
avoidance/denial technique, seek to label us "obsessed with being Gay." But we
know that our self-affirmation will be trampled upon if we do not bring the rich-
ness of our experience to bear upon every life situation and interaction. We are
impatient because of the suffering of our sisters and brothers and find it hard to
endure the footdragging pace of "liberal" response within the church. We seek
to speak truths that the people we address do not wish to hear. But we must
keep talking, keep affirming, keep living and sharing our lives with dignity and
integrity. Only then will the truth of our lives and the truth of our movement
undeniably emerge. And only that truth will liberate the church from its homophobia and enable it to become truly inclusive.

THE MEANING OF FAITH

It is difficult to imagine that the son of a carpenter and a teenage mother, a man who declared himself to be the Son of Man and was acclaimed as the Son of God, had any intention of founding an institutionalized religion. It is more probable that Jesus of Nazareth, whom we Christians affirm to be the Christ, intended to enable an experience of genuine community united in the experience of God's inclusive love. The community he called into being by his style of life was characterized by faithfulness, response-ability, and caring. He enabled persons to share their meanings. He encouraged persons to take responsibility for their own lives, to acknowledge their relatedness with God, and to be responsive to the lives of others. He gave women and men, girls and boys a personal experience of God's love, acceptance and forgiveness. He called persons to be real in his presence, to forsake pretense and to enter into communion with him and with each other.

The Community of Faith was and is a community of persons bound by faith in covenant with God and with one another. Persons entered the community of Christ-followers because they responded to the life and teachings of Jesus and because they had personal faith in the truths he revealed. It is our response to the life of Jesus and our affirmation of Jesus as the Christ that enables us to respond to his call to discipleship. In responding to his call, we enter into communion with all who have dared to take the name of Christ with conviction and commitment.

The early members of the Christ community filled the catacombs with joy-full singing and welcomed the opportunity to witness to their faith in the arenas of Rome—such was their confidence in the love of God and the assurance of grace, the unconditional presence of spiritual empowerment. They had partaken physically and spiritually of the presence of Jesus the Christ and, according to their faith, had responded to the truth he revealed. It was their faith, not obedience to any moralistic or legal codes, that was and is the essence of their and our identity as Christians.

Faith is a profoundly personal, internal affirmation of an unseeable, untouchable and unprovable truth. When a person identifies with the Community of Faith, she/he is expressing a personal internal affirmation. Declaring Jesus to be the Christ is an act of faith. No one has the moral prerogative to challenge such a response in another person. Because we cannot enter into another's life experience, feelings, or encounters with God, we cannot judge the validity of another's affirmation of faith. At most, we can only witness the meaning that another's faith holds by witnessing the manner in which she/he relates to other persons.

Nevertheless, throughout history the church has challenged—even denounced—the faith responses of many who have identified with the Community of Faith. In order to maintain control, the fathers of the church (the mothers of the church having been obliterated) wrote creeds designed to separate the believers from the nonbelievers. Purported to be affirmations of faith, such creeds (Nicene, Apostles', etc.) were primarily designed to keep certain persons out of the Community of Faith. Christianity became a credal religion of the state. Its doctrine became entrenched. Its institutionalized patriarchy became increasingly more reflective of cultural and social prejudices and decidedly less responsive to God's interaction with humanity and humanity's faithful response. It remains so today.

Yet it is essential to understand that persons are still called into covenant relationship with God and with one another. We respond according to our faith. This fact remains true in spite of an institutional church that is more concerned with doctrine than with faith. Gay people who have remained within the institutional church, even though we have more than adequate reason to abandon it, have remained because of our faith. We remain because our affirmation of Jesus as Christ requires us to respond to the covenant community he sought to enable. We are called to live in community with all who dare to take the name of Christ, even those who strive diligently to deny us our right to live freely in that community. Though many of our Gay sisters and brothers look upon our religious faith as more of an affliction than an attribute, we continue to respond to the call to discipleship. We live with the hope that the institutional church will rediscover its identity as a Community of Faith.

Christ came to redeem, not to judge. His was a redemptive, not a legalistic or moralistic ministry. Having been nurtured in the Jewish faith, Jesus surely understood the Jewish legal codes and moral admonitions. Indeed, according to the record, at the age of twelve he sat teaching the elders of the synagogue. It is unlikely that he would have been given a hearing had he not been speaking of the time-worn precepts of the Jewish faith. Surely the Gospel he later proclaimed would not have received such a hearing.

His deep understanding of the Jewish tradition gave meaning to the Good News which he as the Christ came to personify and proclaim. By his own admission, according to the record, he came to fulfill the law and to bring to the consciousness and personal experience of women and men a new understanding of God's interaction with humanity—a new covenant. He came to proclaim that the spirit of love has superseded the law. Every interaction in the life of Jesus attests to this fact. He taught that treating others as we would wish to be treated is the primary meaning of the law and the prophets. He defied Jewish law and the customs of his time in order that the Gospel of love might be made manifest. He taught and healed on the Sabbath, he spoke publicly with women, he associated with outcasts and related to Samaritans. He never married and he encouraged people to forsake their families and become his disciples. According to the record, he gave warnings of condemnation to only three groups of people—the wealthy, the keepers of the law, and the leaders of the religious establishment. Clearly, he came to convey a deeper understanding of God's will—a redemptive, not a legalistic/moralistic understanding.

We of the Community of Faith respond to the creation of a new covenant between humankind and God. Christ-centered faith proclaims that through the death and resurrection of Jesus, God inexorably and absolutely bound her/himself in covenant with humanity. It is a new covenant from which no person is excluded. As a Christian, I believe that in Jesus the Christ, God took upon her/himself human flesh to personify her/his will and to make visible the meaning of the divine/human relationship.

The response to God in Christ is a response of free will—not to an absolute code of moral admonitions but to a dynamic, personal experience of the inclusive love, forgiveness and grace (the spiritual empowerment) of God in one's own life. My experience as a Gay man in a hostile society has often been an experience of separateness—from God and from other persons. For many years I believed it was necessary to hide the fact of my Gayness, thinking that doing so would overcome the separateness. I lived with pretense, related to others with deception and denied my experience of love. In doing so, I denied the power of God in my own life.

Slowly I came to the realization that in every encounter during his earthly life, Jesus invited persons to abandon pretense, to take responsibility for their own lives and to acknowledge their relatedness with God and with one another. I believe God reveals her/himself to those who acknowledge the insufficiency of their self-sufficiency, who abandon pretense about who they are, and whose bearing toward their sisters and brothers in the human community is characterized by caring, forgiveness, respect for her/his dignity and affirmation of her/his sacredness.

Ultimately the meaning of faith is reflected in the lives of those who know in the depths of their being that God's inclusive love embraces them as they are. Such was the love personified by Jesus the Christ. For me, as a Gay man, it has meant coming to understand that the deep love that I experience and express toward other men is the love of God revealing itself in and through me. So rich and full of meaning is the experience of that love in my life that I am able to embrace myself and others with honesty.

My response to the new covenant revealed by Jesus the Christ and my identification with the church—the Community of Faith—are given in free will. In acknowledging my relatedness with God, I necessarily acknowledge my relatedness with all persons. To dare to take the name of Christ demands that I share the Good News that God's inclusive love embraces each of us as we are. It demands that the truth of Christ be proclaimed: forsake your pretense, take responsibility for your own life and do not fear your experience of love. It is God revealing her/himself in your life.

PUTTING PAUL INTO PERSPECTIVE

The Gay men who identify with the Christian Community of Faith do so because of our fundamental affirmation of Jesus as Christ. We are Christians, not Paulists. This distinction is important because the church has relied heavily on the writings of the Apostle Paul to support its condemnation of Gay people. (See Robert Treese's article, Chapter 2.) It has done so with a total disregard for the hermeneutic, or interpretive, perspective. The liberal church has traditionally viewed the Pauline epistles, which are culture-bound and time-caught, as being open to interpretation at every point *except with regard to passages which refer to homosexual acts.* This inconsistency in itself demonstrates the homophobia of the church. But beyond that, Paul himself clearly provides hermeneutic guidelines. His writings reflect a conscious and clear distinction between that which he believed to have been imparted to him by God and that which he himself believed to be true. In every reference to same-sex relationships, Paul makes it apparent that he is expressing a personal judgment.

Paul's writings must be understood within the social context of his time and place. The influences of the Greek culture, a predominantly homosexual culture, were empirical realities. Paul found the Greek culture personally threatening and no doubt considered its intellectualism antithetical to Christian faith. Paul's concern for the continuation of the Christian community in a pagan world dominated by Greeks and Romans certainly contributed to his prejudice against homosexual acts, since the prevailing society openly tolerated them. And he no doubt genuinely believed that homosexual acts were contrary to the will of God, having been reared in the Jewish tradition that condemned all sexual acts not related to procreation.

We must also understand Paul's unique theological perspective. His early writings clearly reflect his expectation that the Parousia, the second coming of Christ, was imminent. His entire perspective was colored by his belief that during his lifetime Jesus would return to usher in the Kingdom of God. Consequently, Paul's writings are replete with admonitions to the Community of Faith: Do nothing that will interfere with your relationship with God; the Parousia is at hand. For this reason Paul felt that celibacy, not heterosexual marriage, was most in keeping with God's will. (This is an interesting contrast to the Old Testament affirmation of polygamy.) With the passage of time, Paul realized that he had misjudged the Parousia. His later epistles, particularly to the Thessalonians, reflect his new understanding of the meaning of the life of Christ.

Paul judged homosexual acts without taking into account the emotional and psychological motivations for them or the quality of relationships they express. He knew nothing of variant sexual orientations. He condemned homosexual lust, as do most Gay Christians. He apparently knew nothing about Gay love, or, if he did, he was terrified of it (a posture not unusual for one reared in the Jewish tradition). His belief that homosexual acts were idolatrous (a rejection of the created order and of creatureliness) was uninformed by our contemporary knowledge that same-sex relationships exist throughout the created order. In fact, the exact opposite of Paul's view is true. Sexual union between persons of the same sex is an affirmation of the created order. It is an affirmation of the variant forms of sexual expression ordained by God and a celebration of the fact that human beings experience and sexually express love in a variety of ways.

Throughout his writings, Paul implies that people who engage in homosexual acts implicitly refuse to recognize their relatedness with God. He sees those acts as symptomatic of paganism. Burdened by his Jewish history, Paul found it impossible to understand that a person can in fact affirm the Christian faith and also engage in homosexual acts. His limited comprehension is consistent with his shallow understanding of human sexuality in general, a fact about Paul which should not be overlooked. Paul's image of God as withholding grace is inconsistent with the nature of God revealed by Jesus the Christ. Clearly, Paul's primary concern is in denouncing paganism. Equally clear is the fact that he was greatly confused concerning the relationship between paganism and homosexual acts.

We must not ignore the essence of the Good News Paul proclaimed. He believed that the passion, death and resurrection of Jesus the Christ were central to an understanding of human freedom. In Christ, and in the response of faith to the Christ event, personal liberation becomes a reality. God's love embraces human life, alleviating *all* distinctions and granting to mortals victory over sin and death. Pauline theology thus affirms the inclusive nature of God's love though often Paul himself lost sight of its meaning. His essential message is constant: Freedom comes to people who make the response of faith to God's decisive interaction with humanity.

These facts will not be accepted by persons who hold dogmatically to biblical literalism. They maintain that the Bible is verbatim the "word of God." They ignore the facts: the Bible was inspired by a feminine Holy Spirit, written down by men, and edited and translated several times. With each edition and translation the text was doctored (though, the literalist might argue, this work was certainly inspired by the Holy Spirit), and the cultural prejudices of the transcribers were incorporated into the text. Moreover, the original biblical texts were written without punctuation, leaving phraseology and quotation markings to the prejudicial discretion of translators and editors. Also, the twenty-seven books canonized as the New Testament were but a handful of a mass of literature that existed in the early church. We can speculate upon the motivations of the early church *fathers* who decided which books would be canonized. Surely their decisions, grounded in good will, were influenced by cultural realities and concern for ecclesiastical power.

At best, biblical literalists inevitably find themselves burdened with contradictions—to be expected when one is dealing with a book written, edited and translated over the course of several centuries. At worst, literalists become so occupied with the *words* of the Bible, they fail to comprehend the truth it consistently conveys concerning the constancy of God's love. The Bible has profound significance as an historical and literary record of God's interaction with humanity and the revelation of God's will. When it is used to substantiate personal prejudices and self-righteous judgments, as it often is by literalists, its importance is diminished.

A belief in biblical literalism is symptomatic of a person's failure or inability to exercise free will. The literalist betrays a fear of taking responsibility for her/his own life, decisions, and the consequences of those decisions. As long as there is an "absolute" (though clearly contradictory) listing of "dos" and "don'ts" to which one can profess to give allegiance (though no one has ever completely succeeded in doing so), one need not use one's own intelligence or manifest one's own faith. Blind allegiance to the biblical word is a denial of personal responsibility in relationship with God and with neighbor. Therefore, biblical literalism can in fact be declared to be idolatrous. It is a rejection of free will which is irrefutably a gift of God. Literalism is antithetical to the responsible life to which Jesus the Christ called his followers. It is also a denial of the continuing revelation of the Holy Spirit.

Of course, there is really no such thing as a pure literalist. There are only selective literalists. Those who use certain (edited and translated) passages from Paul's epistles as proof that God condemns Gay people are selective literalists. Their irresponsible use of Paul's writings gives evidence to their inability to cope with the reality of Gay love and Gay people and perhaps more often their inability to cope with sexuality and/or their own Gay feelings. Their homophobia, not their faith, is revealed.

HOMOPHOBIC ARGUMENTS

The church has historically perpetrated the myth that Gay people are inherently sinful because of our sexuality. The sexual expression of Gay love has been condemned because it is deemed to be "unnatural." It is said to be contrary to God's will because it does not serve the procreative function. It has been made criminal because the church continues to give credence to the manufactured belief that homosexuality had something to do with the destruction of Sodom and Gomorrah. Gay people are thought to be incapable of love, slaves to lust, abandoned by God and rightfully spurned by the church. All oppression of Gay women and men is founded upon such mythology. The mythology is rooted in homophobia: fear of the same (here relating to gender and sex).

The fact that same-sex relationships have been found to exist in every species of animal testifies to the fact that the created order includes homosexuality as a normative form of sexual relating. To contend that only heterosexuality, and no other experience or expression of sexuality, is God-ordained is to project limits on God as Creator and is contrary to all that Jesus revealed concerning the nature of God. Human beings are endowed with the gift of sexuality—that is, with the potential to relate sexually with other human beings, regardless of gender. Sexual orientation—the *primary* emotional, psychological, erotic and social responsiveness experienced by human beings—is socialized by a wide variety of influences, including but not limited to human interaction, environment, and emotional experience. Through the socialization process human beings acquire a sexual orientation—bisexual, homosexual or heterosexual. All these orientations are normative and equally conducive to the sexual expression of love. God's purpose for humanity is revealed in love between persons—female/female, male/male, and female/male—not in denials and repudiations.

There is no justification for the belief that God has limited the transcendent experience of sexual love to persons of opposite sexes, married to each other, and relating sexually in the classic "missionary position" (woman on bottom, man on top). Yet the institutional church has endorsed and perpetuated precisely such a belief. Surely love characterized by mutual respect, responsibility and honesty— love that is rich with joy and meaning—is not alien to God's will and/or purpose.

The fact that Gay relationships have the same potential for fullness as heterosexual relationships is a threatening reality to the church. Acceptance of this idea would require the church to undertake a total re-evaluation of its attitudes toward sexuality in general. Quite simply, it would have to admit it has been wrong about a great many things over a very long period of time.

For instance, the proposition that sex has value only for procreation is the pivot for most of the church's attitudes on the subject of sexuality. But even heterosexuals are no longer accepting this cruelly narrow point of view. Modern contraceptive techniques—truly unnatural phenomena, every one—enable heterosexual couples to relate sexually with a fair amount of certainty that conception will not occur. Thus they are free to experience and express other meanings in their sexual lives. Sexual relationship is the most intimate form of interpersonal expression and the surest communication of caring. Beyond this fact, procreation becomes a matter of personal responsibility for the heterosexually relating couple. It becomes a matter of personal choice, hopefully made with an understanding of the seriousness of parenthood. If and when the choice is made, procreation itself becomes an expression of love, not an affirmation of creatureliness as some, harking back to Paul, would have us believe. But it is absurd to think that a person must have the experience of mothering or fathering a child in order to be fulfilled. People are fulfilled by experiencing love in relationship—female/female, male/male, female/male— love characterized by mutual honesty, respect and responsibility.

The church has done a profound disservice to humanity by insisting that the only function of sexual relating is procreation. Too often conception is accidental, unwanted or resented. Too often pregnancy is used as a means of manipulating or exploiting. Too often women and children become victims of men whose sense of self depends upon virility demonstrated in procreation. How much better it would be for humanity if such men truly understood the nature of caring. How much more life-giving it would be if the church were to emphasize the expressive and communicative dimensions of sexual relationship and put the procreative function of sexuality into its proper perspective.

The procreation-only position is basic to the argument that Gay sexuality is anatomically unnatural. The argument goes like this: The vagina was designed to accommodate the penis (as woman was made to accommodate man), and the intention of God is clear in this regard. To deny anatomical reality is ridiculous. The interaction of the sexual organs serves the purpose of procreation. Therefore, these organs exist solely for the purpose of procreation.

This argument underestimates God's benevolence toward us. To insist that God ordained only one purpose for the human sexual organs is to project a limitation upon God based on a personal value judgment. Such a judgment is grounded in a basic fear of sexuality. It indicates in those self-appointed judges an unwillingness to take responsibility for their own potential in sexual relationship. When we consider the multiple functions of other parts of the human anatomy (even the other physiological functions of the genitals), the single-purpose view of the sexual anatomy is shown to be inconsistent. Human sexual anatomy does serve the procreative function; but this is but one of several functions, not the least of which is physical union between persons who love each other, regardless of their genders.

Further, human experience does not verify the anatomically unnatural argument. A significant and growing number of heterosexual persons are engaging in anal/genital and oral/genital sexual activity to express their love and achieve mutual gratification. Indeed they have been encouraged to do so by every contemporary marriage manual designed to enable greater meaning in their relationship. They have recognized that human beings can relate sexually in a variety of ways, all of which are natural and healthy. But the church by and large still tries to inspire guilt—and even horror—at the very idea that such variance might exist.

Gay and non-Gay people engage in essentially the same sexual activities. It would be prejudicially dishonest to deny this fact. Would the church maintain that certain sexual acts are acceptable in the female/male relationship as long as the vagina and penis are eventually united, but unnatural under any other circumstances? Are relationships to be judged on the basis of genital interaction? Is this not relegating the essential meaningfulness of human relationships to a strictly physical (genital) plane? Is it not more important that the couple of whatever genders relate in ways personally meaningful and expressive of their caring? Is not the quality of the relationship of primary concern?

It is a fact that persons of the same gender can experience fulfilling, selfless love and that they have an inherent right to the full expression of that love. The church must understand that this very love has for centuries made it possible and continues to make it possible for Gay persons to endure oppression. The church oversteps its authority—and does violence to the spirit of the one who came to bring abundant life—when it judges the love of millions of Gay women and men to be sinful.

THE GOOD NEWS FROM GAY LIBERATION

Through relationship with God and with other persons, female and/or male, each of us experiences the fullness of our divine/human nature. Relationship is the essence of the created and the social order. It is within relationship that persons experience human fulfillment. Fulfillment is made possible when both people care for each other, feel equal with each other, are honest with each other, are willing to communicate, have respect for each other, and embrace their responseability which is enhanced as time goes on by the continual growth of each person. Gender simply has nothing to do with fulfillment.

One more factor is necessary to fulfillment and relationship: That is the integration of sexual feelings with the expression and communication of the enabling attributes just listed. The internal erotic response of one person toward another, irrespective of gender, is fulfilled when it is expressed integrally with these attributes. And when this integration takes place caring is deepened and greater sexual fulfillment is experienced. Fulfillment in sexual relationship, then, is an integrative, interpersonal, growing experience.

There is a distinction to be made between sexual *relationship* and sexual *relating*. When sexual feelings and not abiding love are physically expressed by mutual consent sexual relating takes place. Sexual relating between mutually consenting persons may or may not be manipulative and/or exploitative. When it is—that is, when abuses of human interaction take place—the relating is rightfully denounced. Relating based on manipulation and exploitation gives unnecessary pain, violates dignity, and alienates, and is therefore sinful. But sexual relating which is devoid of manipulation/exploitation and which affects only the persons who are relating by mutual consent must not be denounced. Sanctions against sexual relating between mutually consenting persons violate the personal right to privacy and the God-given right to exercise free will. There is no harm in sexual relating per se, and no sin. It is distinct from fulfilled sexual relationship but represents a mutuality on the part of those relating which causes them to reject manipulation and exploitation as styles of relating. Respect for one another's dignity is affirmed.

Gay people, as a matter of survival, have often been forced to isolate our erotic feelings from the other dimensions of our personhood, so we viscerally understand the difference between sexual relating and sexual relationship. For many generations, we have been told that we are incapable of experiencing a meaningful sexual relationship. Many of us have been conditioned into believing that our only means of sexual expression is sexual relating. Until the emergence of Gay consciousness, the fact that thousands of Gay people were experiencing sexual relationship was not widely known. The majority of Gay men believed that they were incapable of sexual relationship but were capable of sexual relating, so the latter became their essential pattern of sexual expression. But today we know that sexual relationship as an integrative, interpersonal, growing experience is a true possibility for all of us. We have known the reality of sexual relating and the fragmentizing of sexual feelings. And many of us know the reality of sexual relationship because we have, in our deeper understanding of who we are, learned to affirm and integrate our sexual feelings with the relational attributes that make possible a fulfilling relationship. We affirm that both sexual relating and sexual relationship can be meaningful when manipulation and/or exploitation do not occur.

We also know that most human beings of every orientation engage in sexual relating. Many do so with the expectation that sexual relationship will follow. It is possible for sexual relationship to evolve from sexual relating. There is overwhelming evidence of this fact inside and outside of the Gay community. Many marriages, for instance, which begin as sanctioned sexual relating evolve into sexual relationships. While the institution of marriage, with the cultural, familial, social and religious support it enjoys, might enable some sexual relating persons to develop a sexual relationship, and thus experience fulfillment, it is not essential to that development. Thousands of Gay women and men are fulfilled in sexual relationships without the sanction of marriage or familial and social support.

I have noted earlier that the church has traditionally maintained that sexual relationship and fulfillment are possible only within the context of marriage—particularly when procreation results. The church would do well to acknowledge that marriage, as a legal institution, really functions only to protect the economic interests of the people involved. The inequitable, discriminatory function of marriage as a legal institution in providing inheritance rights, joint ownership rights, and tax benefits should be openly denounced, not only by Gay persons, but by all non-legally-married (and dissatisfied married) people.

The essential theological understanding of marriage is that it is a covenant relationship. This understanding is justifiable as long as the making of covenant is a privilege/responsibility equally available to persons of any gender who desire to enter into covenant with one another because of their love. There is a profound need for a rediscovery and reiteration of the meaning of marriage as a covenant relationship. By participating in such a rediscovery the church would come to recognize that it has the privilege and responsibility to celebrate covenant love relationships between any persons regardless of gender. The blessing of the Community of Faith can and should be given in joy and celebration to covenant love relationships entered into by two women, by two men, or by a woman and a man.

Further, the church must recognize that covenants are meaningful only when they are entered into freely. Greater meaning is to be found in a covenant defined by the covenanting persons than in a contract or a list of obligations imposed upon them from without. The church should celebrate a covenant that grows out of a fulfilling relationship. It should acknowledge with great respect the commitments that each party is willing to make to the other in the presence of God and the Community of Faith. Hopefully, such commitments are made because of love—not because of a sense of obligation or social or religious pressure. In order to protect against destructive elements in relationship, the covenant should be renewable at the will of the persons who have entered into it.

The family is an extension of the covenant relationship. At least two forms of family structure bear consideration: the nuclear family and the extended family. The nuclear family is one in which persons are related by blood or by legal definition. Members of a nuclear family, with the exception of the mother and father, are not there by choice but by birth or by legal action. The nuclear family is patriarchal in its structure and self-understanding. As it exists today, the nuclear family bears little resemblance to the biblical image of the family as an emotional and spiritual support to the entire community, characterized by faithfulness, openness and hospitality to persons in need.

The extended family, in the contemporary meaning of the term, is composed of persons who freely choose to relate to one another, whether or not they are related by blood or legal ties. It is not limited by size or geographic proximity. The commitment and love that exists between persons, and the element of free choice, not legal obligation, are the definitive elements. The interaction between persons and the meeting of individual needs through multiple interpersonal relationships is central to the extended family. Openness to and affirmation of the sacredness of individuals is central. Members share in the interpersonal, interdependent life of the extended family because of their love. Individuals relate as family members because of the quality of their relationships, and the making of commitments to one another, either formally or informally, within the extended family enhances those relationships.

Because interaction with a variety of persons occurs in extended family relationships, all members experience a greater degree of fulfillment for their personal needs without placing excessive demands upon one another. The Gay parent (and there are many) who has retained custody of her/his child(ren) inevitably establishes a relationship with her/his child(ren) that is characterized by a degree of honesty not even approached in most nuclear families. The circumstances of life and the reality of oppression require such honesty. Interaction with the extended family encourages the mutual growth of all persons involved. Such interaction enables each family member to understand her/his own uniqueness, needs, abilities, and possibilities to a greater degree than is possible in the patriarchal nuclear family, simply because there are more persons with whom to relate and from whom response to one's own self can be experienced. And, quite obviously, the nuclear family serves the negative purpose of the patriarchal society and church in perpetuating a limited view of human relationships and of sexuality.

Gay people experience pain in the nuclear family system that insists upon a narrowly defined understanding of relationship and sexual expression. We are primarily concerned with the quality of familial relationships, and freedom for all persons, particularly children, to discover who they are in a secure, affirming, honest environment of love. We try to foster an understanding of life that is inclusive and nonprejudicial. The relative freedom from sex-role socialization that exists within most Gay families enables children in those families to mature in accordance with the uniqueness of their individual personhoods. Gay people know that a person's fulfillment as a human being is not dependent upon the attention of the opposite sex or involvement in a nuclear (heterosexual) family. Most important, children grow up knowing that sexuality is a beautiful part of life, that each person has the right to her/his own feelings and that what is important is that each person learn to relate to others withcut manipulation or exploitation. In short, children growing up in Gay families learn to value the quality of relationship and the primacy of love, without regard to gender.

The essential attributes of a healthy family are equality, honesty, caring, willingness to communicate, mutual respect, and response-ability—the same attributes that make any fulfilling relationship possible. In the patriarchal nuclear family these attributes usually do not exist because of the inherent inequality built into the structure. Heterosexual persons who readily accept the one-partner/nuclear family style of life usually have not confronted their own potential in human relationships. They accept the nuclear family model and the fidelity to a single partner primarily because they have been conditioned to do so by society and the church. Too often they enter into marriage because of personal insecurities, frightened by the thought of remaining single in a society that values marriage as a measure of success. Too often they have not explored their individual identities as sexual persons. They become what they are expected to become, investing little time or energy in trying to discover who they uniquely are. This lack of self-knowledge is directly related to the difficulties many heterosexual couples experience in the emotional, psychological and physical intimacy of marriage. Such couples have not acted freely in the truest sense, although they believe that they have chosen the style of life they are living.

Gay people, living as we do in a hostile society, have been forced to examine our relationships and our style of life. We understand the need for primary relationships. Yet when we limit ourselves to sexual relationship with only one person (though all persons have the capacity to experience sexual relationship with more than one person) we do so out of love and free will, not because society and the church have imposed a limitation on us. We do not believe the society or the church has the authority or the right to restrict and direct the divine/human experience of love.

Contrary to social myth, then, great faithfulness can characterize Gay relationships and does in a majority of cases. But our fidelity is an outgrowth of
our love, not a response to social or religious expectations. There is an essential health in our style of life because we are responsible for and to the
relationships in which we are involved; we are not bound by legally or socially determined codes of behavior. In the context of social and religious
oppression in which we live, the health in our relationships is a source of
great strength to us. As loving women/loving men, we have experienced a
fullness in life that gives us reason to rejoice.

ANDROGYNY AND HUMAN LIFE

To be Gay involves more than sexual orientation. It also involves acceptance
of the androgynous (gynandrous) nature of human life. The emergence of
Gay consciousness has enabled us to understand that our uniqueness lies in
the fullness of our feminine/masculine personhood. Consciously and subcon-
sciously we reject the strictures of sex-role socialization and open ourselves
to the fullest possible experience of who we are by affirming both our femininity and masculinity. We experience ourselves as integrated and complete
feminine/masculine persons. As we bring the gift of our integrated androgynous personhood to human interaction, we open ourselves to the possibility of
interpersonal wholeness.

Bisexuality, which may well be the most natural sexual orientation, is reflective of the androgynous nature of human life. The ability to relate freely
to persons of either gender might well be the essential nature of all of us. But
our society and the church do a thorough job of conditioning us to repress
our bisexual potential and express ourselves heterosexually. In the lives of
Gay people, the conditioning toward heterosexual expression is contrary to
our essential feelings. To expect or require Gay people to live heterosexually
is to compel perversion. The truly perverted person is she/he who denies her/
his truest feelings and seeks to relate sexually in ways that are alien to her/his
essential emotional, psychological, erotic, and social nature.

During the struggle to understand and affirm our sexual identity, we who
are Gay become aware of our bisexuality. But acknowledging our responsive
feelings toward persons of the opposite sex does not necessarily require us to
rethink or feel insecure in our sexual identity. There is simply no reason to
force those feelings of responsiveness to overt sexual expression. It is contin-

gent upon each individual to understand her/his deepest sexual feelings and to express those feelings responsibly. It serves no purpose to violate one's true primary feelings in sexual expression for the sake of bending to the status quo (of church or society). What is of importance is that we are aware of our bisexual essence. Of equal importance, for us and for all people, is our right to self-definition and the freedom to act upon our *primary* feelings.

Most heterosexual persons, and especially heterosexual men, have a very different response if they are aware of their bisexual essence. They fear their responsive feelings toward persons of the same sex and overcompensate in demonstrating their heterosexuality, flaunting it in order to feel more secure in it. Their fear is based upon an ignorance or denial of the bisexual nature of life and of their own androgynous nature. Instead of experiencing the fullness of their personhood that androgyny allows, they desperately try to prove the significance of their masculinity by scapegoating Gay people, by "beating up queers." Behind many condemnations of Gay people is the fear of androgyny. Our presence disturbs others by reminding them of their own androgynous feelings.

So, again, a truth demonstrated by Gay people in our day to day lives makes it obvious that the church must squarely face the facts of human sexuality. Perhaps the understanding and acknowledgement of androgyny in the created order is the primary point of all those I wish to make, the point most relevant to the church. For the image of God is, in fact, androgynous: feminine/masculine are united in each mortal life. Feminists and Gay people are declaring this truth to the church with growing urgency. The male-dominated church has failed to comprehend the essential nature of God. Its theology, its language, and its structure —in short, its sexism—violate the essential nature of God. Feminists and Gay people are calling the church to the urgent task of dealing with the theological, social and personal consequences of affirming an androgynous God, revealed in an androgynous Christ to androgynous women and men.

THE LIBERATION OF THE CHURCH

Implicit throughout this chapter has been my firm belief that the liberation of the church depends directly on the courage of Gay men within the church to step out of the closet, with faith, into the full light of self-affirmation. As Gay men within the church, we are in a time of testing. Faith urges us to proclaim our truth and our experience of the love of God. Fear holds us back. Ultimately,

we must come to terms with our freedom in Christ and grasp our freedom within the Community of Faith by acting free.

We are called to share in the movement within the church that will serve to
liberate the church from its homophobia and sexism. But the closet door opens
only from the inside and often it opens very slowly. Each Gay brother must open
the door according to his own conscience, willingly taking the risks of living with
faith, not fear. The time has come to leave coat, tie, and heterosexual mask at
home. The church is the one community in society in which we have a responsibility to be real. We are called to be real in one another's presence. We may do
so without fanfare in the lived experience of personal interaction. We may choose
to openly share with the Community of Faith our self-affirmation. In whatever
way we elect to share our truth, we must do so with forthrightness, with full
honesty, and with love. In doing so, we will help to open the doors of the church
to all persons. So long as the majority of Gay men within the church participate
in the conspiracy of silence, for whatever reasons—job discrimination, fear of
ostracism, or the inability to truly embrace our selves—the heterosexually-oriented
church will remain ignorant, fearful and prejudicial.

It is particularly important for Gay men in positions of power—denominational executives, program agency executives and staff persons—to be honest about
their Gayness and to expose the absurdity of attitudes within the church. Their
responsibility is greater because with power comes influence in the patriarchal
structure. But the self-affirmation of every Gay man in the church is important.
Persons in the Community of Faith must have the opportunity to viscerally encounter openly Gay persons at every level of the church with whom they can
enter into dialogue. Human interaction is the most effective weapon against
stereotypical and mythology-laden attitudes. Persons must be enabled to confront their prejudices in order to learn that their attitudes have limited their
growth and that they—not we—are the true victims of homophobia and sexism.

The liberation of the church is long overdue. The time has come for the church
to be held accountable for the violence it has done to our dignity and to our experience of love. It is time for the church to be true to its mission of liberation.
Gay men must be the vanguard of the movement within the church. Working
with our Gay sisters and with all persons within the church who are victims of
the church's homophobia and sexism, we must engage in the ministry of education and advocacy. In the Spirit of the Gospel we must declare in no uncertain
terms that the time has come for the church to:

1. Affirm Gayness as a variant form of sexual experience/expression that is ordained by God as a natural part of the created and social order.

2. Affirm Gay relationships by providing an environment in which Gay people experience respect, acceptance, and the affirmation of dignity.

3. Welcome Gay people into the church with joy, encouraging us to share our lives fully, freely, and openly in every aspect of the church's life, and make certain that Gayness is affirmed in publications, from the pulpit, etc.

4. Encourage the growth of Gay relationships by fostering free association among Gay people within youth groups, young adult groups and couples' groups which provide social opportunities to church members.

5. Recognize the importance and uniqueness of Gay perspectives by electing Gay persons to decision-making bodies and to offices within the church.

6. Provide opportunities for persons to interact with Gay persons and discuss the ignorance and mythology which is the foundation of homophobia.

7. Make available resource materials that communicate the truth about Gayness and Gay people—preferably materials written or prepared by Gay people.

8. Provide materials and funds for the re-education of ministers, pastoral counselors, and other church professionals with regard to Gayness and Gay people.

9. Screen all curriculum in churches, church-related schools and institutions and seminaries to guarantee that a truthful, affirmative portrayal of Gayness and Gay people is being presented.

10. Require seminaries to institute and require courses related to Gay concerns, including courses on counseling Gay people and on confronting collective and personal homophobia.

11. Encourage Gay people to enroll in seminaries and provide scholarship funds to them, recognizing that they have been victims of discrimination in employment which often causes economic distress.

12. End all discrimination against Gay people at every level of the church including admission to seminary, ordination, and employment. Every local church, regional body, program agency, and denomination should declare a no-discrimination policy in regard to sexual orientation and/or marital status.

13. Seek federal legislation to guarantee protection of the civil rights of Gay

women and men and end job, public accomodations, and housing discrimination based on sexual orientation and/or marital status (by amending
Title 4 of the Civil Rights Act of 1964).

14. Work for the repeal of all laws which make the sexual expression of Gay
love criminal.

15. Work to end discriminatory law enforcement and to end police policies
of enticement and entrapment to harass and arrest Gay men.

16. Work to end discrimination against Gay people in the armed services, in
civil service, and in the granting of security clearances.

17. Allocate church funds to pay legal costs in significant court cases that
could result in positive precedent-setting decisions.

18. Provide meeting space and resources for Gay organizations and groups.

19. Celebrate covenant relationships between Gay persons, developing litur-
gies that are inclusive with respect to gender and which give affirmation
to same-sex relationships.

20. Develop a totally new theology of sexuality which would reflect the validity of same-sex relationships as well as other relationships and life styles.

21. Examine the assumptions and positions currently held concerning marriage,
family, sex-role socialization, abortion, contraception, and other concerns
related to sexuality.

22. Respond to the pastoral needs of Gay ministers who are heterosexually
married as well as to the needs of their spouses and families; respond to
the special needs of parents of Gay persons.

23. Affirm the health of extended family relationships and support the right
of Gay persons to retain custody of children and to adopt children.

24. Do all within its power to end social and cultural prejudice against Gayness and Gay people by anti-defamation efforts and by serving as watch-
dog for violations of the rights of Gay people, false portrayal of Gay
people in the public media and subtle forms of discrimination.

25. Guarantee our right as Gay persons (and that of all persons) to define
ourselves and to speak in our own behalf whenever our lives or rights
are being discussed or violated.

26. Facilitate organizing efforts by Gay people in the church as well as within society, and provide forums for us to present our understanding of who
we are and to share the meanings of our lives.

27. Support efforts by Gay persons to serve the needs of the Gay community
recognizing that many sources of funding are not open to us because of
the prejudice of society.

Being Gay is a blessing in a society that consciously teaches men not to
love one another. We know the joy, meaning and beauty of the male/male
relationship. We know the health of being free from the male stereotype/
mentality and the perverse effects of homophobia. We know the importance
of affirming our androgynous selves.

The church has been and continues to be our greatest oppressor. Let us
speak from within—presenting our demands with honesty and faith—mindful
that whenever new truths emerge from within an institution, they surface
slowly and painfully. Our love will endure the pain and will enable others
to endure the pain. The church will resist mightily because we are calling it
to be transformed. Fear and hatred will surface and will be directed at us and
all who join us in the struggle. It will not be a new experience. We have experienced the fear and hatred of others all our lives. It is time for us to join
hands and confront it directly. Our love is stronger than the fear and hatred
of those who will oppose us.

And when we are truly heard and the struggle is over, we will share in a
resurrected Community of Faith that lives in light instead of darkness and in
which love between persons—female/female, male/male, female/male—is affirmed
and celebrated as sacred.

When I began
work on this book I knew I had not yet
clarified—much less fully resolved—my conflict
with the church; but I was not prepared
for the experience that came with writing
"The Miracle of Lesbianism." It has been a time
of pain and growth for me. What resulted is an
attempt to reconcile my feelings as a Lesbian
and as a woman with my Christian history.
The process of writing was bodily and psychological
just as much as it was intellectual. My physiological
systems and my moods fluctuated in grand
empathy with the rhythms of the writing.
Thanks to this process and several caring and
clear-thinking women
who criticized, edited and discussed
the paper with me, I now feel richer and a
lot more self-understanding than when I began.

The chapter
is not finished, and I doubt that it ever could
be. On the one hand it tries to do too much
and on the other it neglects some vitally
important issues. I am aware that I did not provide
an economic framework for all the considerations
discussed; nor did I link up Lesbian
identification with other liberation struggles.
Nevertheless, I hope this chapter raises questions
and opens the way to dialogue, particularly
among women and particularly among women who
have been or who are Christians.—S. G.

THE MIRACLE OF LESBI- ANISM

SALLY GEARHART

INTRODUCTION

You are a woman who loves women. You are, as Del Martin and Phyllis Lyon describe her, a woman whose "primary erotic, psychological, emotional and social interest is in a member of her own sex, even though that interest may not be overtly expressed." (*Lesbian/Woman*).*

It's difficult for you to be an active member of a Christian congregation. Particularly if you are a single Lesbian, it's hard to hear mother's day sermons, to go unescorted or unfamilied to the church picnic, to relate to the ladies' auxiliary when there's no man to whom you're an auxiliary. But you may not be a single Lesbian. You may be married or divorced or separated or widowed, for you come in each of these varieties, too. Whatever your marital state, it is

*See the Selected Bibliography for full bibliographic information.

isolating to be both a Christian and a Lesbian. With whom for instance could you possible share, at the funeral of a woman you've loved, the depth of the life you had together?

You brace yourself to go to weddings, and frequently when you get there you hear that passage from the book of Ruth drifting from the lectern or choir loft: "Entreat me not to leave thee . . . ." You remember how these words were originally spoken between two women, and it is bitterly ironic to you that they are used to sanctify heterosexual unions while you can never say them in a service like this to the person you love.

It's not surprising, you think, that so many thousands of Lesbians have left the church. You wonder how many thousands more there are like you who remain within the institution. And you wonder where they all are, and why they don't scream their rebellion against the pressure they must feel unremittingly. Then as always you remember why you yourself do not rebel. You weigh again all that you've got to lose and then you wrap your rage and your pain in the cloak of Christian endurance and you put a smile on your face and make yourself sit docilely in the pew to watch your friends get married

The church never asks you who you are because it doesn't want to know. Were the subject to come up, you'd become a sort of accidental attachment to the category of "homosexual," which means, to both church and society, *men* who relate to each other sexually. The question of women's loving women has always taken a back seat to the question of same-sex relationships between men, and it still does. Only one of the mentions of homosexuality in the scriptures suggests "Lesbian acts": "Their women exchanged natural relations for unnatural" (Romans 1:26).

Why is this the bible's only direct reference to "Lesbian activities"? Why are Lesbians of so little comparative importance in the scriptures? The answer is as painful as it is obvious. Lesbians are women. According to the Judeo-Christian tradition, women are less important than men; they are in fact as the language of the quoted passage makes clear, the property of men: "their women." There was no reason for Old Testament writers to mention sexual activities among women. After all, in woman-to-woman sexual expression the property relationship between a man and his wife presumably was not endangered. No seed of Israel was spilled upon the ground in a waste of potential progeny, that is, property. Hebraic law simply did not concern itself with relationships among the less-than-human things like houses, servants, asses, oxen and wives. We also observe in passing that if Hebraic code had accorded women full human status—that is, if it had considered women to be part of "mankind" as some would argue that it did—then Leviticus 18:22 might emerge as a sanctioning of Lesbian sexuality: "You shall not lie with a man as with a woman; it is an abomination."

Paul's reference, though the only scripture condemning woman-to-woman love, has nevertheless been important to Lesbians. One quotation is all that is needed. It has helped to make society's accusation of the Lesbian explicit; so that if and when the question of female homosexuality arises, the proof of her "sinfulness" is right there in Romans 1:26. Furthermore, Paul's mention of woman-to-woman love exclusively in the context of sexual expression has supported the myth that the Lesbian is *only* a sexual being, that she is to be defined as "a woman who has sex with other women."

Society at large and the organized church in particular, need to hear the following message. As Lesbians we deny the "sick-and-sinful" definition that has been laid upon us. We are emerging from the fear and isolation resulting from that definition. We are in our rising consciousness concerned for all women across all societally inflicted barriers—economic, racial, religious, age and "sexual." We are bored by the apparently titillating male fantasy that describes us only by our sexual practices. We indict the Judeo-Christian tradition not only for its inhumanity to Gay people but for its dehumanization of women. Finally, we urge that anti-life tradition—that church—immediately to collapse into the living of the gospel. We can begin to articulate these things through an exploration of the following categories:

    A. *Lesbians/Women/Feminism*
       Lesbians/women together in conditioning
       Lesbians/women separated by rebellion
       Lesbians/women reunited through feminism

    B. *The Christian Tradition's Hatred of Lesbians/Women*
       Its direct expression
       Its obliteration of history
       Its perpetuation of sex-role socialization

    C. *Lesbians/Women/Feminism in the Church*
       Feminism's incompatibility with the church
       Feminists surviving in the church
       Feminists leaving the church

LESBIANS / WOMEN / FEMINISM

Lesbians/Women Together in Conditioning

In the beginning of our lives, the woman who is called Lesbian and the woman who is called heterosexual stand on the same ground of experience. In the United States, Lesbians have been brought up together with our heterosexual sisters—often blood sisters—in heterosexual families to be heterosexual women. Both of us, Lesbian and heterosexual, heard the shade of disappointment in the doctor's voice when he said, "It's a girl." We both registered on some level of consciousness that our baby brothers were tossed higher and played with a bit rougher than we were. We both dimly recall that the toys most likely to be visited upon us were dolls and tea-sets instead of trucks and tools. Lesbians just as commonly as other women saw our mechanical and mathematical abilities sink into disuse and near oblivion just about the time we began to learn how important it was that we "catch a man."

We were together consumed with concern for our appearance—perhaps even bought our annual quota of thirty tubes of lipstick together—and together we wobbled hand-in-hand into adolescence in those high-heeled, life-limiting shoes. With our heterosexual sisters we absorbed the subtle messages that women enjoy being raped, that we are naturally suited to housework. Wide-eyed together we heard Hollywood, TV, the recording industry, in fact all of Madison Avenue, describe us as sexy/pure whores/virgins—and if we were confused, we got it all perfectly clear on Sunday mornings: Helpmeets, that's what we were, helpmeets to the Crown of Creation. And virgins, of course, make the best helpmeets since they are undamaged goods—that is, having known no other they are likely to be content with the man they get.

Lesbians were instructed right along with our heterosexual sisters in the mating games that meant our survival as women. Together we endured the embarrassment of the chivalry that would put us into the lifeboat first. Together we've understood why we're encouraged to spend lots of time on our backs where we're helpless. Men of influence like Nietzsche, Napoleon, and Luther branded all of us from birth as mere breeders, and Freud told each of us how our neurosis lay in our failure to accept the fact that as women we were simply inferior beings. Nobody asked us whether we were Gay or heterosexual when—in the name of Jesus Christ, if you please—they drowned, tortured to death, or burned alive nine million of us as witches.

Both heterosexual women and Lesbians have been the target population of a system that teaches us to be "vessels" for men. The sex-role socialization that began so early for all of us is a many-levelled phenomenon. Any attempt to explain its functioning or effect will inevitably be full of seeming contradictions, over-generalizations, and half-truths. Nevertheless, the attempt has to be made.

To oversimplify a very complex situation, then: Sex-role socialization is the practice of programming male people into patterns of creativity, rationality, independence, violence, objectivity, dominance, toughness, action, adventurousness and competition; and the programming of female people into patterns of receptivity, irrationality, dependence, nurturance, subjectivity, submission, gentleness, passivity, domesticity and cooperation.

The sex-role model assumes that women and men are "half-persons," each of whom possesses certain specific traits and each of whom needs the traits afforded by the other in order to become whole. There are positive traits possessed by both women and men and both women and men possess negative ones. So, the nurturance associated with women and the independence associated with men are both "good" things, while a woman's passivity or a man's violence is "bad." The hitch is that the qualities *most* valued by society somehow happen to be those accorded to *men* while those *least* valued are laid upon *women*. Society thus most affirms such qualities as intellect and objectivity and least affirms such characteristics as irrationality and submissiveness. Moreover, in every case of a positive value wihin the societal view of women, the parallel male virtue is just a bit better. So receptivity and being able to listen are of course "good"—it's just that action and articulateness are a little bit better; domesticity is not "bad"—it's just that adventurousness is more appealing.

The "helping" professions perpetuate the myth of the half-person, and perpetuate as well the comparatively devalued and adolescent status of the woman. In one study—and there have been many such—both female and male psychiatrists, psychologists, and social workers were asked to choose the characteristics that they would ascribe to (1) the mentally healthy male, (2) the mentally healthy female, and (3) the mentally healthy adult. The result was that the healthy male and the healthy adult were described by essentially the same characteristics, while the healthy female was described by a totally different set of words. Such terms as active, objective, aggressive, worldly, leader, direct, and confident were used to describe males and adults. For the female such terms as dependent, passive, subjective, sneaky, conceited, easily hurt, and follower were used.[1]

Apparently society feels that to be man is to be grown up, but to be woman is to be something less than man, something less than adult. So, it's not surprising that a woman seminarian I know was told that her psychological profile test showed too many "masculine," i.e., adult, characteristics. She was referred to a psychologist for "help" so that she might cultivate a more docile (less grown-up, more dependent) demeanor. There, of course, she was told that she'd never be happy until she shed her "masculine" ways and became more "feminine."

What society wants from us as women seems to be a matter of what men do not want for themselves but need to have provided somewhere in their environment: the "feminine" which is also the not-quite-adult. A man, having neither the awareness nor the courage to find and affirm the "woman" inside himself, must do so vicariously by conquering a woman who allegedly has exclusive possession of the qualities he needs. She becomes his womanness for him. What society wants from men, on the other hand, seems to be a matter of what men want *exclusively* for themselves: "masculine" characteristics. A woman, having neither the position nor the power that would allow her to express the "man" inside herself, attaches herself to a man, to a person who has society's permission to be "masculine," to be "adult," to be her manness for her.

And so it goes on: a world of alienated half-persons seeking their full selves "out there" in a member of the opposite sex when all the while they are their own wholeness. Real humans are not half-persons but women and men who are each in themselves made up of all the positive and negative qualities presently assigned by society to either one sex or the other. Moreover, what is human is an affirmation of the woman-associated traits which carry positive value (but which are still slightly-less-than-the-best in society's eyes). Finally, what is human is a tempering of some of the deified "masculine" values—like objectivity and logic—which have been revered to the exclusion of their opposites. These deified qualities threaten the health of individual men, the health of some individual women, and the survival of us all. They threaten us not because they are "masculine," but because they are exclusive and extreme. There is nothing inherently destructive about logic or objectivity, but attached to an attitude that says only these characteristics are to be appreciated, they become a rampant tyranny. They lose all proportion and become anti-life.

If we had to fight the battle against sex-roles only in ourselves or in those close to us we might conceivably make some headway against them. But the task is far greater than that. Sex-roles have become institutionalized. What happens to the individual woman and to the individual man is recapitulated in a societal dimension. The jobs that require the characteristics accorded to men (such as strength, initiative, adventurousness, leadership, intellect) are mostly filled by men (physical laborers, astronauts, military officers, doctors, lawyers, politicians). Similarly, the jobs that require the characteristics accorded to women (such as nurturance, domesticity, relatedness, gentleness, followship) are mostly filled by women (wife/mother, teacher, nurse, domestic worker, switchboard operator, clerk/typist).

Further, the jobs that women have are not "bad" and certainly they are essential since they are the maintenance tasks of the society, the jobs that keep the system running. Women have the jobs that produce and maintain the producers (the men). Yet the jobs that men have are always *more* respected than those women hold, and the experts even in "a woman's field" are consistently men (Dr. Spock, Paris designers, chefs, educators, supervisors). In this way the images of the half-person and of devalued womanness are magnified and intensified on a grand scale. Any individual who attempts to escape from the sex-role in her/his own life must defy an entire system.

We have absorbed into all of our societal structures and into our whole outlook on life this division of qualities into "feminine" and "masculine." We have absorbed, too, the subtle superior evaluation of the traits that happen to be associated with men. All women—heterosexual and Lesbian alike—have internalized to a great or small degree the myth of the half-person and the assumption of male superiority which implies our own inferiority. Accordingly, our self-image and our very lives are poisoned by self-hatred.

Lesbians/Women Separated by Rebellion

Though we've shared a lot with our heterosexual sisters of what at the kindest can be called oppression, there are differences between us, points at which we diverge radically in our experience and in our feelings. These differences are not so much innate as acquired. They are related to the degree to which and the manner in which heterosexual women and Lesbians have responded to the sex-role conditioning of our society.

The Lesbian is that woman for whom the conditioning to one degree or another was not successful. In loving other women she says "yes" to womanness, to herself as a woman. In speaking this "yes" to herself, she speaks a "no"

to society. She is the woman who has rebelled against the male society's definition of her. To the extent that she rebels against this definition—which renders
her an object or a vessel for men—a woman can be called a Lesbian.

She says "no" to the wife role, and unless she is forced to it through economic necessity, she says "no" to prostitution. The only other alternative
allowed her by society (that is approved of and supported by men) is that of
the virgin—"old maid" or "spinster." Again, as with "wife" and "whore,"
these words identify her in terms of her relationship to men. As it happens,
most Lesbians (75 percent by most estimates) have had heterosexual experience.[2]
(Some Lesbians would say that they have thus made their choice of life-style on
more relevant evidence than have their heterosexual sisters.)

The Lesbian denies all three of the male definitions of women. Her "no" to
society is grounded in a "yes" to her own self-identification, to her identification as a woman, to her identification not by men and for men, but by and
for the women she loves, and most particularly by and for herself. The term,
"virgin," then, may still be a good one for the Lesbian—if and only if the original meaning of the word is restored. In the ancient sense, "virgin" means "one
unto herself." The wholeness implied by that description is what Lesbians with
growing consciousness are seeking.

Speaking of the Lesbian's rebellion against sex-roles brings us dangerously
close to the naive yet explosive question so often asked of Lesbians and of
Gay men: "What 'causes' homosexuality? " It is a naive question because it
ignores the controversy that has raged for decades about the "cause" of any
personality trait or behavioral characteristic. It is explosive because it implies
that there is something wrong with Gay people, that there is some "sickness" in
them to be "cured." Outraged Gay people point out that a more intelligent question is "What causes heterosexuality? "

Sexuality researchers (the Kinsey Institute, Johnson and Masters, etc.,) have
concluded that human beings are born just plain *sexual.* People at birth have
the capacity to extend themselves to others of either sex; they are healthy,
wholesome human beings capable of loving and relating to other human beings.
Except for the practice of imposing sex-roles, there would be no need to use
the prefixes that label the human being as *"homo*sexual," *"hetero*sexual," *"auto*-
sexual," or *"bi*sexual." Sexuality or being sexual is a natural capacity to express
and to receive love and affection.

Exclusive heterosexuality has to be understood as a perversion of this natural

state. We very quickly rob infants of their health and wholesomeness. We require them at birth to fall into one of two widely differing and oppositely valued categories: girls and boys. We further require them to obliterate half their loving nature so as to become lovers *only* of a member of the opposite sex. It is as if at birth without our knowledge or consent we are injected with a heavy addictive drug that will assure our limitation to one sex role and to exclusively heterosexual relations. We're hooked early. We're heterosexual junkies. When we become adults, we push that drug ourselves, not just on other adults and children but on every newborn infant. To kick the habit is near impossible.

Why Gay people broke free from the addiction, no one can say. In the case of the Lesbian, she may have had parents who let her develop human (that is, by this society's standards, manlike) characteristics instead of limiting her to those of girl or woman. Perhaps she and her Gay brother inherited a disposition to freedom. Perhaps the stars were right. We cannot cite causes. We can only say that through some amazing strength or good fortune, the Gay person resisted the drug that would have sent her/him down the path of exclusive heterosexuality.

We cannot say when, anymore than we can say why, the Gay person chose to resist or why the resistance lasted, or what factors throughout her/his life ebbed and flowed and vied with each other so that she/he emerged wishing to invest herself/himself in a person of the same gender rather than in someone of the opposite gender. It is hard even to talk of the heterosexual person's "choice" to be heterosexual. For the woman, marriage and/or man-relatedness is no choice at all. It is the norm; it is the expected. It is in fact the coerced. Similarly, it is expected that a man will be heterosexual. From the moment our sex is announced every mind and every institution in our environment shifts into one exclusive pattern of relating to us. Women are driven mercilessly to prepare ourselves for men's use, to prepare ourselves as vessels that will be "filled" and given meaning by men. Men are driven mercilessly toward the stud image, toward their destiny as the active principle, the "fillers" of the vessels.

In this light it is not the Lesbian or the Gay man who is "unnatural" but rather the heterosexual person. The Gay relationship moves toward expression not because it is conditioned from birth to do so or because it is approved of by society or because it is given any positive reinforcement whatsoever. Clearly the opposite is true. The motivating energy of the Gay relationship flows rather from inside the persons themselves, from sources that are far more authentic than are responses to external programming. In order for Gay love even to be expressed it must strain against seemingly insurmountable odds. Yet women who love women and men who love men keep reappearing in every society, in every age. This fact alone seems to say something about the chosenness of the same-sex relationship, about its naturalness, about its goodness and about its health.

To return specifically to the Lesbian's experience, perhaps the most we can say with integrity is: The "cause" of Lesbianism is a remnant of self-love that expresses itself in love of other women and thus in rebellion against a woman-hating society. Moreover, the moment a woman *knows* and says to herself that her energy most naturally and most fulfillingly flows toward women, she has exercised for herself the ultimate resistance to her culture. That moment may occur early in childhood, in the teenage years, in the twenties. It may occur after a marriage or even in a woman's seventies—grandmothers have been known to discover their love of women. The Lesbian may articulate the knowledge only to herself or only to a lover. She may allow it to be known—though probably not said—only in the isolation of a small fearful Lesbian community that lives under a threat of disgrace in some bible-belt town; or she may articulate the knowledge to the world with the support of other Lesbians who articulate that knowledge about themselves for all to hear. Whenever it is and under whatever circumstances, she is saying "no" to a system that would define her for others rather than for herself.

The Lesbian is thus a miracle. She is a miracle on two counts: first because she can express her love in the face of thousands of years of condemnation of such experience; second, in a society so steeped in woman-hatred, for a woman to love another woman—for a woman to love herself—is a miracle indeed.

If we are all born with the capacity to relate to both sexes and if the Lesbian has been able to resist at crucial points the conditioning that would make her exclusively heterosexual, then why is she exclusively homosexual? Why doesn't she relate to both women and men? The answer has a distinctly political flavor. Even if after many years of struggle a man were able to be enough like a woman for a Lesbian to love, *still* the fact that men in general have power over women in general has to be dealt with. One social scientist's analysis provides an accurate and succinct answer.

> *(1) [I]n society as it presently exists, there are distinct economic and social imbalances between men and women;*
> *(2) the ability to love can be developed to its fullest*

extent only in relationships between equals; (3) women,
due to the effects of socialization and the present struc-
ture of society, share a basic equality . . . . where women
are concerned, highest development of the ability to
love can occur only in a homosexual context.[3]

So sex-role socialization is responsible—because of their different responses to it—for the separation of heterosexual women from their Lesbian sisters. But the damage done by sex-roles is far more extensive than that. If researchers are right in concluding that human beings are born sexual, and if it's true as the same researchers suggest that to attempt to limit that sexual response is actually physically and psychologically unhealthy, then the reality of sex-role socialization and the tyranny of exclusive heterosexual conditioning will have to be condemned as one of the most alienating, destructive and dehumanizing practices of all time. In all of our hopes of understanding our sexuality, in all of our whispering about pornography, in the relationship of sex and violence, in all of our concern over the ways in which "young people" "should" relate, we have not asked the deeper question—the real question about human sexuality. Could much or all of our sexual repression/violence/alienation be the result of our sex-role socialization? Of the strict limitation of human beings to heterosexual relationships?

Lesbians/Women Reunited through Feminism

The history of the association between Lesbians and heterosexual women has been first a coming *together*—we heard the same messages and even acted together on many of them—and then a moving apart—with Lesbians rebelling alone against exclusively heterosexual sex-role conditioning. The third stage upon us now might be called *reunion,* for beyond the rift created by societal conditioning we share something besides oppression with our heterosexual sisters. We share a potential for and a drive toward liberation. It is a long and hard, frightening and transforming process, and we are forced by it to look at the world and at our own histories in brand new ways. We are drawn together as women by *feminism,* the fundamental ideology of liberation.

I understand that feminism has built into itself a flexibility that makes any definition of it only temporarily applicable. So we begin with what we each feel our own feminism to be and we reach out to others who support and/or alter that understanding, and we constantly in our efforts to speak, make allowances for the changes that speaking itself brings about.

To me, feminism at its most fundamental level is a revolt against the efforts of the dominant culture to alienate life from itself and to destroy life. The dominant culture is patriarchal and masculist—that is, it has spent six to ten thousand years perpetuating the myth of male superiority. It has sanctioned male virtues, denied women's participation in them, and emphasized them to the point of deification. It has done all this for the purpose of maintaining material and psychological power not only over women but over any subdominant culture within its reach. The tool of the patriarchy most useful in keeping its control intact has been sex-role socialization.

To me a feminist is a woman—and very occasionally a man—who is growing in three ways: *in woman-identification, in psychological consciousness,* and *in political awareness.*

To grow in woman-identification is to say "no" to definitions by and for men; it is my continuing effort to define myself. It is to love and trust myself in spite of a world that has taught me to hate and to mistrust myself. That world has, in fact, historically expended its greatest energy teaching me to hate and mistrust all women. To be woman-identified is to give energy and care to myself and to other women; it is to affirm in myself those qualities that have been called with derision "womanly," and thus second-rate—qualities such as emotionality, receptiveness, intuition, and nonlinear thinking. It is furthermore to affirm in myself those characteristics usually confined to men, like intellect, creativity, energy, logic. It is to deny the myth of the half-person, to expose the myth of "pure objectivity," and to affirm all human characteristics as potentially expressive of myself. It is particularly to assert that "truth" lies in relationship and process rather than in competition and product. Whatever a feminist "naturally" is, she embraces as ultimate the healing and life-sustaining values of empathy, flexibility, awareness, receptivity, and responsiveness.

To be woman-identified is to suggest that men have their own wellsprings of strength and do not have to drain us of our precious woman-energy; they do not have to lean eternally upon us—upon our groundedness—for their existence. It is to say that we are tired of being buffer states of conciliation between men; that they can either find love and care within themselves for each other, or they can continue without us down their accelerating conveyor belt to destruction. The fact that they are taking us with them down that path makes it even more urgent that we identify with every breath not only *with* women but *as* woman; we must recognize and embrace in ourselves the life-giving and life-sustaining parts of nature. These parts have been buried a long time by masculism, both in men's individual selves and in the patriarchal culture. The time has come for all of us, both women and men, to woman-identify.

To be growing in psychological consciousness is to ask the question immediately and for the long run, "What am I doing? " It is to function in the world out of self-knowledge and not out of response to competitive stimuli. It is to acknowledge that while the world boasts of logic, objectivity and premeditated order, the great preponderance of all human action is irrational, subjective and spontaneous. It is to commit myself to acting not out of logic alone and not out of irrationality either, but out of a deep and expanding *knowledge about* my irrationality. This means being aware of who I am and of who I have been. It means reflecting upon the things I have done so that more and more I can close the time gap between action and understanding. I can begin to know what I am doing *as I do it.*

Psychological consciousness requires that I ask questions about leadership and collectivity, professionalism and authority, about hierarchical structures, about how to do away with power relationships. It requires me to examine my own power and to learn how it is that I have power over others and they over me. It requires me to attempt to give up using other people or being used by them through such power. My psychological consciousness makes it necessary that I do not govern others and that I become self-governing in the most profound sense of that term. That self-governance is then the starting point for collective action.

Growing in political awareness is essentially the process of linking up my suffering with someone else's so that together we can make it all stop. To grow politically is to identify my own pains and to be aware of other people's pain. Through political awareness I become able to separate the experience of other people from my own and still see in what ways the source of our pain is a common one, in what areas our pain coincides, and at what junctures we can join hands to alter reality. To be growing in political awareness is to stand on my own ground, on my womanness and on my woman-love—for I am not of color and I am not poor and I can stand only where my roots are. I stand there and learn from there about the ground that other women stand upon. It is to listen to and to feel with other oppressed peoples. It is to learn how to remain connected to my history and to my whole self as I move toward action and change in my own environment and ultimately on an international scale. Finally, to grow in political awareness is to struggle with the knowledge that even as a woman I have some power and privilege if I'm educated and/or white; it is to de-guilt myself for having such power/privilege and yet to be wary of my own opportunism in a system that seeks tokens and offers me tempting comforts at the expense of others.

The tasks of becoming woman-identified, psychologically conscious, and politically aware are not easy, nor are they accomplished quickly. Often in the process our rage is so deep or our needs are so great that we cannot wait for our own growth or for the far-off solidarity we envision. If we grow too impatient, we lose ourselves prematurely in isolated acts of rebellion. Often we are alone when we cry our agony, alone when we steal food for our children, alone when we break into uncontrollable hysterics at a cocktail party, alone when we sell ourselves literally or figuratively to the highest bidder in order desperately to prove our "worth." We are alone because sisterhood is a process and a dangerous one at that. It won't happen overnight, and all along the way commitment gives way to fatigue, while care and mutuality backslide into mistrust and self-aggrandizement. So in our isolated rebellion we are jeered at or called names ("castrating," "crazy," "woman's libber") or we are fired from jobs, given extra duties, imprisoned, strait-jacketed, beaten, drugged or lobotomized. We refuse to adjust to the dominant ideology of annihilation and we rage against it with all the anger and love of life that we can muster. We can no longer afford to do that alone.

We begin the tasks of feminism by taking risks and by reaching out to each other. We learn woman-identification through sharing; we are supported in our self-knowing by others who begin to know themselves; we learn about the a-b-c's of economic reality through dialogue and unified action as well as through individual study. We cannot do it together without pain, but it will not be done at all if we try to do it alone.

We have been trying for several years to articulate the difference between Lesbians and other women. We have had trouble drawing a dividing line, perhaps because there is in fact no line to be drawn. Certainly there is no sexual line. A substantial number of Lesbians have never sexually expressed their love, and a substantial number of women experimenting sexually with other women while maintaining the heterosexual privilege they have by relating to men, cannot be called Lesbians at all. We do not become Lesbians by leaping into bed with another woman. We don't "become" Lesbians at all. Rather, we simply discover that we can and do love women.

Somewhere along the way, every Lesbian said "no" to a system that would define her in its own exploitative manner. She may not call herself a feminist. She may not even be openly a Lesbian, but if she loves and affirms herself and other women, then she strains steadily toward feminism. In the present world-wide atmosphere of moving women, her straining in that direction seems irrevocable.

The woman who calls herself heterosexual is still saying "yes" to an important part of masculist identification. It is vital that she begin the task of letting herself love herself and other women. That is difficult to do while relating to a man. It's vital that she direct her primary energy toward women. That is also difficult if not impossible to do while relating to a man. When she does turn her energy away from men and toward women, when she does turn her sexual expression away from men (note: *not* that she necessarily turns her sexual expression *toward* women) then she sweeps toward feminism as irrevocably as does her Lesbian sister.

Instead of thinking of Lesbians and heterosexual women as daring each other to cross over some artificial line that divides us, we should envision all of us as attempting to reach out to each other with common needs and realizations. As we grow in our understanding of our feminism, we are propelled toward each other in what is fast becoming a history-changing process. Feminism is thus the link, the potential ground of unity for the heterosexual woman and the Lesbian. Sharing the soil of feminism, women can consider the question of Lesbian love in a new context, and explore it in ways that expose traditional views of Lesbianism to be narrow, shallow and not at all to the point.

Any woman who seriously moves toward self-identification, toward woman-identification, with all that that implies about rethinking her understanding of and feelings about men, seems clearly to be approaching the Lesbian life-style. If she's really woman-identified, she'll be glad to be called a Lesbian, whether or not she's ever experienced what the patriarchy would define as the *sine qua non* of Lesbianism: a sexual relationship with another woman. Lesbianism is a mind-set, a life-style, a body of experience. When it is tempered by the fires of feminism, it is also the most formidable political posture that can confront the dominant culture.

THE CHRISTIAN TRADITION'S
HATRED OF LESBIANS / WOMEN

Its Direct Expression

The church—the institution, its doctrine, its believers—has expressed its woman-hatred, its Lesbian-hatred, in a number of ways. The most blatant manifestation is in its canonical dictates, the "nos" enunciated by ancient Hebraic law or based upon that law, and the suggestions and subsequent interpretations made by New Testament men as to what women's place should be. Negative attitudes emerge more from the remainder of the New Testament than from the gospels; Jesus' behavior and teaching demonstrate an unusual respect for women, at least according to the extant gospel material.

Any concordance will provide reference to the things that the men of the Hebraic tradition or the apostle Paul would not suffer from women. We have only to remind ourselves of the Romans 1:26 indictment of sexual expression between women; of the Orthodox Jewish prayer that daily thanks god that the pray-er is not a woman; of the fact that Augustine and other church fathers debated about what part of a woman's nature was redeemable, and whether or not she could possibly be redeemed by being transformed in heaven into a man, or if indeed she was redeemable at all. We need only to observe the structures and methods of local churches to witness the continuation of these traditional restrictions.

We have only to look at our legislative bodies, our government, our court system and at our medical profession to see how tangibly the long arm of the church reaches into Lesbians'/women's lives. In an effort to rescind and revoke recent gains for women in abortion legislation and court decisions, tens of millions of dollars are at this moment being poured into political efforts by churches, particularly by the Catholic church. Heavy church pressure is being applied to Christian (particularly Catholic) congressmen, and an amendment to the United States Constitution is even being proposed. In the eyes of the church we have no right not to bear children; on the other side many of us—usually poor and of color—are sterilized without our consent by white doctors who make that decision for us, about our bodies, about our lives. California legislators wave the bible and quote Leviticus against the decriminalization of sexual acts common among all adults, heterosexual and homosexual alike. Unwed mothers are robbed of their children by courts that are deaf to the realities of love and creative growth but which nevertheless hear the uptight moralistic whispers of the church. The collaboration of church and state, of church and professions, in the oppression of Lesbians/women is clear enough to be considered a conspiracy.

The Obliteration of History

Perhaps more important and certainly far more subtle is the fact that Christian men—and women too by complying with the myth of male superiority—have conducted a frightening obliteration of women's active and creative part in history both before and during the patriarchy. It has happened over thousands of years. It is difficult to trace, since it is not in the interest of masculists to encourage our seeking out the material and the knowledge that could undermine the patriarchy. But that this obliteration has indeed taken place is a blatant testimony to the Lesbian/women hatred built into and perpetuated by the church.

A growing number of scholars now speculate that prior to the patriarchy—that is prior to all we know of recorded history—the world was in the hands of woman-run cultures, matriarchies and gynocracies about which we do not hear precisely because the first task of the patriarchy was to obliterate all traces of the existence of these cultures. (Consult Davis, *The First Sex*; Diner, *Mothers and Amazons*; and Mellaart, *Catul Hüyük* in this regard.) The complex way in which this whole expanse of pre-history was reconceptualized, rewritten, and totally altered is perhaps best demonstrated by recent research and speculation surrounding the accounts in Genesis of the creation of the human species. We are aware of at least three substantially documented variations of the creation story—two of which are in Genesis itself. The third has emerged from cabalistic writings—unorthodox tradition which does not have the official sanction of the patriarchal church.

An accurate translation of the Hebrew word for god (*Elohim*) in the first Genesis narrative (1:27) posits her/him as an androgynous (a gynandrous) being, having both sexes complete within her/him.[4] She/he creates woman and man together as equals. This narrative seems compatible with what we know of the transition between female and male cultures when goddess worship was on the way out and male-god worship was emerging.

The second Genesis narrative (2:21-23) presents a male god all the way. The great goddess has yielded to Yahweh. The he-god first creates a masterful man and then a subservient wife, the paradigm for the male dominance of the next ten thousand years or so. To be sure, traditional biblical scholarship, if we can

afford to trust it, asserts that the second of the two narratives was written before the first. Certainly there is a scholarly (and a psychological/political)
rationale for the patriarchy to claim that the masculist god is more primitive;
Genesis 1:27 may thus have to be considered a "throwback" to matriarchal
times rather than a transition from them. At any rate, new findings and new
interpretations suggest at least that the myth of creation is richer than and
different from the picture painted by the patriarchy.

The third and most appealing story, from unorthodox Hebrew tradition,
may help to explain any incompatibility of the Genesis passages. In it, god
creates Lilith and Adam as the prime and equal couple. Lilith deserts Adam
because he insists that she "lie in a recumbent position." Adam complains to
god and god then makes Eve, a more docile partner who will presumably obey
Adam (Graves and Patai, *Hebrew Myths*).

Even psychology—traditionally the enemy of women—now begins to rein-
force our suspicions. Theodor Reik suggests that since myths recapitulate
physical and psychic realities, it was Eve who was primary, and Adam was
born from her and became her lover and husband (*The Creation of Woman*).
A Jungian interpretation, given credence by the work of Erich Neumann and
Joseph Campbell suggests that the loss of primacy of the culturally "feminine"
principle is expressed in the second Genesis narrative.

We must admit the possibility that there's been some tampering with history
in our Judeo-Christian heritage, and once we do that, questions come thick and
fast. We have to ask why the Lilith story was omitted and why god ended up
male. Further, whatever the order of their writing, why has the second Genesis
version extolling man's superiority over his mate traditionally been given pre-
cedence over the first version in which the two are equal?

Once we begin asking these questions, we are forced to re-evaluate every
interpretation of history and every article of our faith. We have to look again
at the fact that the major figures presented to us and elaborated upon in bible
and church history are almost exclusively male. Occasionally to be sure, there's
a token woman of whose noteworthy activities much is always made. Usually
she is in relationship to a man in the role of wife or mother. We have to read
very carefully or dig very deep in order to realize that Deborah, for instance,
led an army—or that Jerome lived surrounded by virgins whom he considered
equal to himself in spirituality. (Did these virgins love one another?)

The church has denied our capacities and hidden all reference to them. To the woman-identified-woman, to the self-conscious Lesbian, discovering pre-patriarchal history is an experience of affirmation never given us by the church or by society. It helps us to understand why the church could never affirm us as women or the love relationships that sustain us as Lesbians. It helps us to understand the fear that has made the church so oppressive of any woman who threatens to be a whole person. The research suggests that at one time in history to be a woman was to be woman-identified, that is, self-identified—and that all women then were what the conscious Lesbian is striving to be to-day: a self-loving, intelligent, capable, caring, energetic, full person, independent of men and masculism's standards and definitions.

The Perpetuation of Sex-Role Socialization

The third expression of the church's hatred of Lesbians/women is in its dog-matic stress upon sex-role socialization and upon its companion structure, the nuclear family. Religious bodies, and particularly Christian ones, are our most up-front pushers of the sex-role habit, of the daddy-mommy-baby habit. They peddle the drug daily.

Pick up any church publication to find examples. One has on its cover a "mother of the year" teaching eager children from a book whose central char-acter (a boy) is saying, "Thank you for this good meal, Lord, and bless Mother who must now wash the dishes." The same publication is full of the faces of the white men who keep the business going—except for the "Kitchen Korner" in which "the girls" share a "prize-winning recipe." Any educational or wor-ship material, any doctrine, meeting, function, ceremony of the church makes painfully clear the line of authority: from God-the-Father through the instru-ment that is Mother Mary, to the Son with all his brothers and (only presumab-ly) sisters. The immediate concern of the church seems to be to keep girls girls, boys boys, and father comfortably seated above them all so that we may be constantly reminded that in the home as in heaven the highest authority is testicular.

The tyranny of the nuclear family can continue because most people be-lieve in the myth of the half-person—because mothers have been taught since they wore pink bootees that to be a mother in such a family was their desire and their destiny; and because fathers are pressured throughout their lives to compete and achieve so they can be fully responsible for the lives of two or three or four others in exactly this pattern. Daddy, mommy and children, along with other parallel units, then comprise the cells of the body that is the church.

The oppressive familial organization of the church is brought into bold relief by the plight of the Lesbian in one simple, seemingly casual, circumstance: With whom does she go to the church picnic? Well, if she's lucky there's a Gay man around who is as willing as she is to have a "front." If they do not "know" about each other, this can at best be an anxious occasion. The Gay man is usually worried that she might suddenly become interested in him; he thus ventures toward her only half-heartedly in his effort to look like but not be a potential husband. The Lesbian, on her part, usually makes lots of nervous references to the other men in her life or feeble jokes about her commitment to spinsterhood. If they "know" about each other, and if both have some theatrical flare, then the occasion can be an artistic performance, full of fun and delight for all parties.

Perhaps if there's no Gay and/or single man around, the Lesbian can attach to another single woman or to a group of single women who have learned to live with being thought "peculiar"; but that circumstance is rare too since single women, if they exist in any numbers, tend not to trust each other enough to gather together with ease. After all, manhunting, or even the pretense of it, is not a group task.

If the Lesbian is exceedingly bold, she can go to the picnic with a Lesbian friend or lover, but only if both of them are adept enough at flirting with men to take suspicion off themselves. Care must be exercised however as every good Lesbian knows, not to flirt too much lest she be thought *too* heterosexual, that is, "loose," and therefore a threat to the sacred bonds of matrimony. Usually she goes alone or legitimizes herself in an "aunt" or "big sister" role by attaching to a family and being very busy playing with the children (does she dare join the men playing softball?) or dishing out potato salad so that matchmakers feel less guilty about her presence.

Any individual failing to fall into the nuclear family pattern is considered within the church to be either on the way to it ("he's such a good catch some girl will get him yet"), justified by having been through it ("well, at least she's got her grandchildren . . . "), or worthy of our condescending love even though she or he is a teeny bit weird—dare we say "unnatural"? —in life-style. The familial organization of the church at best disapproves of and at worst condemns Lesbians, unmarried women, unmarried women with children and married women without children (it must be *her* "fault"). Among women the church sanctions only the married mother, though she too experiences contradictions and emotional conflicts about her faith and her role as a woman.

All single Christians, among them many Lesbians, must somehow work out their salvation not only in fear and trembling but in isolation as well. They have to understand their faith and Christian action without the tangible or psychological supports afforded to a member of a family. We can only imagine what the struggles with salvation and Christian practice must mean to married Christian women, often with children—and there are many of them—who are only now discovering their Lesbian identity.

The paradox is plain. Within a church so bound up in masculist history, in family structures, in the necessities of authoritarian relationship, and in the limitations of "girl" images and "boy" images, faith and action hardly reconcile with being a woman—much less with being a Lesbian.

LESBIANS / WOMEN / FEMINISM IN THE CHRISTIAN CHURCH

Feminism's Incompatibility with the Church

The sooner we articulate it the better: The Christian church by its very structure and by the very assumptions on which it is founded is in direct, fundamental, and irreconcilable conflict with feminism. By "church" I mean both the institution *and* the body of believers who stake their faith on patriarchal theology's most complex and successful mystification: the unique divinity of Jesus of Nazareth and the precepts thereunto attending. In both its structure (hierarchical, authoritarian, competitive) and its theology (extreme and exclusive masculism) the church is committed to the annihilation of life-giving and life-sustaining qualities and to the subjugation of women and of womanness.

The structure of the church is authoritarian and hierarchical. The very identity of the church hangs utterly upon the maintenance of a vertical power-over order. Being ruled by someone above us—ultimately god—is seen as our natural state. The "power-over" prepositions lie in the pattern: god *up* there and the ministers *under* him who stand *above* the laymen who are the heads *over* their wives and who with those wives stand *on* children. Take away this structure and the church would not be the church.

This vertically structured institution is backed up by hundreds of thousands of tinier units of authoritarian control—nuclear families—which embrace the same philosophy and pass down the same values within themselves as are visited down upon collective "mankind" from heaven: obedience, judgment, guilt, punishment, competition, success/failure, ownership of people as property and even "sin-for-the-sake-of-salvation." No amount of insistence that Christian love has transcended deuteronomic law can outweigh the tangible evidence of the world's experience of Christianity. "Authority" has long since skipped over the line into "authoritarian." While love may be mouthed from the pulpits, law still runs the church. Through the power-over mind-set and the structure of the institution, the priority of law over gospel is unshakably maintained.

We are not just dealing with hierarchical structures that exist out in the world. We are dealing with a mind-set, a way of thinking about ourselves and others. It is the mind-set behind the hierarchies that is devastating and that dehumanizes us. Someone must be "better" to someone else's "worse," someone must have "more" to someone else's "less." It is as old as the patriarchy. This mind-set and its institutionalizations have persisted through history in spite of the efforts of people like Jesus to level hierarchies and change our habits of thinking (the "last" and the "first," sitting at the foot and at the head of the table, doing "unto the least of these," etc.). It is the power-over mind-set that has raped and exploited the earth, that lurks behind sex-roles, racism and the profit motive. It is this mind-set that keeps us alienated from and protective of ourselves. It keeps us in fear of one another. It guarantees that there will be wars and rumors of war.

In our brainwashed addiction to the ways of the church and the family, we either crane to look up to those above us or we preen over and condescend to those below us. The church encourages us in these exercises with every suggestion of "worship," "sin," "charity," "heaven," "judgment," and "grace." So steeped are we in this vocabulary and in the dominance relationships that such words represent, that we have trouble articulating any alternatives to such terms, to such relationships. Words like "equal" or "egalitarian" or even "just" or "non-power" simply do not express the human relationships we hope for because they derive their meaning from comparison to hierarchical structure. It is not strange that many feminists are seeking a whole new vocabulary and some a whole new language.

In the growing consciousness that feminism requires, the whole question of power and the use of it is central. Feminism hopes for an obliteration of "power-over" relationships. Feminism leads us to a pattern of collective action void of authoritarian structure. Feminism is based upon personal experience and feelings from which every woman approaches the commitment to share and to work.

Our criticism of hierarchical and authoritarian systems does not spring simply from fanatic rage against the powers that have oppressed us. Our criticism springs rather from a serious and continuing exploration and experimentation with alternatives to authoritarian relationships, with options that do not institutionalize, with models that reduce competitive attitudes. We do not have any answers; but we do believe that there are ways for people to be together which will encourage differences, respect the power of "knowing" something or of having some skill, and allow for leadership, but which at the same time will not require that any person have "power-over" another. We cannot with any part of us understand the ruling of one person by another to be healthy.

Lesbians often feel that our relationships are the beginning of alternatives to power-over associations. In being together without men, we abolish one very prominent power dynamic; and thus we begin to share the sameness of our experience of the patriarchy—sameness against which we can explore our own individual differences. We have some mutual care and some experiential standards with which to examine the games we still play with each other and the clever ways we still try, through our conditioning, to dominate each other. The more conscious we are as feminists, the more earnestly we commit ourselves to the process that will mean an end to our own, and hopefully all exploitative relationships. We expect pain, but we also know what we hope for in our journey to self-love—to woman-love. We feel we have the most sensible, the most nearly equal starting point for that journey: other women. The power-over mind-set which sustains—indeed *is*—the church is utterly incompatible with the new forms we seek, forms that allow for love, trust, cooperation and horizontal relationships.

It is not only the church's authoritarian structure that is in opposition to feminism. Christian theology cannot tolerate feminism either. A very abstract and heady theology comes down upon Christian laypeople. It is visited upon us from the mountainpeaks: our seminaries and the top floors of church headquarters where men have been reasoning for centuries—exclusively men, and exclusively reasoning. We should not be surprised then, that such theology is

very thin. It is not fleshed out at all in fact by any experience save the intellectual. It is a travesty on the gospel, which calls for visceral living experience.
It is in short a theology devoid of humanness because it is devoid of womanness.

We can't remedy this problem by getting more women into seminaries to
"do" masculist theology, for that would leave us even worse off than before.
It would mean that we'd lost more women to the dominant culture. Yet
women cannot "do" feminist theology, at least not in our Christian seminaries, for then it would no longer be Christian theology. A womanization, a Lesbianization of theology is not a reformist move to "incorporate a woman's
point of view." *It is an absolute and uncompromising denial of what has gone
before.*

If this in itself seems exclusive then it's best to admit that is so. But it is
not exclusive out of any hatred of logic or of the abstract or of just "anything male." Nor is it exclusive because we feel the pendulum ought to swing
the opposite way for a while. The pendulum is not at all an appropriate metaphor for what has to happen. Feminist theology is exclusive because it involves
a new beginning, a new starting place, and masculist theology can't be any-
where in sight when that new start is made. We're not talking about the co-
existence of two polarities or some mid-swing compromise. We're talking
about beginning again, about re-sourcing theology and this will change every-
thing. "The bread won't rise if the yeast is still in the springhouse." When in
the process of setting aside our dough to rise we discover that we've omitted
the yeast, we cannot simply add the yeast; we must begin all over again. Or
perhaps a better metaphor is that of razing a building to the ground. Lesbian-
izing or womanizing the "study of god" means beginning down below the
foundations, deep within the earth.

First, male-identification must be denied and woman-identification must be
affirmed. We cannot now be woman-identified within the church any more
than a woman can who gives her energy to a man. Men cannot be helped by
women to find their womanness, nor can the church be helped by women in
that way. The games would simply continue then, and women and men, wom-
en and the church, would continue to be parasites on each other.

The "studying of god" has to come out of experience, has to have base or
ground. It cannot come out of abstract conceptualizing. Concepts and rational
processes will have to wait until we've rediscovered our bodies, our experiences,
our histories and our feelings about all these things. Only then can we connect

our heads with our experiences as the two have never been connected in Christian tradition. The exclusiveness of masculist theology must give way totally to the new and authentic starting point: woman-experience, woman-love, woman-iden- tification. The whole persons that women are becoming—and that men might become if they would woman-identify—can guarantee that such "masculine" qualities as logic, abstract thinking and initiative will not be wiped out of ex- istence. These qualities are also a part of our wholeness as women, and a part of the wholeness of "studying god." But the tyrannical influence they have had in both theology and society must first die completely before they can be redeemed.

The Christian church rests not only upon masculist theology but on ten thousand years of exclusively masculist history and anthropology. This must be put right. But it cannot be rectified within the church. The church cannot afford to acknowledge the matriarchies or to undertake the honest research that would reveal its participation in the atrocities comprising its own patri- archal history. Further, the church and the whole of the Judeo-Christian tradi- tion depend for their sustenance upon the myth of the half-person, upon sex- role socialization and upon the submission of women. Feminism demands that that change. Again, these changes cannot be made within the church.

So the woman-identification that is feminism is impossible within the church. Psychological consciousness, requiring dissolution of power relations, is inimical to church structure, to Christian theology. Too many men (and some women) have too much power to lose. Finally (and this must be examined elsewhere), the political awareness that feminism requires cannot live within the church. Too many missionaries have trampled underfoot too many "heathen" cultures in the name of Christ and capitalism for the church ever to allow an examina- tion of its racism or of its colonial involvement.

It is far too radical for the church—this business of feminism—radical in its proper sense of coming from roots, from groundedness, from experience. Self- love? In the lip service to humility of the Christian church? Never. That part of the commandment—" . . . as thyself"—must be whispered, if uttered at all. Woman-love? In a church which has thrived on male dominance all the way from the second Genesis narrative to the bishop in 1971 who denies women any role but that of receptacle? Not a chance. Non-power relationships? In an institution whose ecclesiastical ladders narrow into phallic steeples? Hardly. Feminism can't live inside the church. The question is: can feminists?

Feminists Surviving in the Church

The hatred of the church for Lesbians/women seems reason enough for all
Lesbians/women within it, once we've understood the situation, to throw off
our brainwashing and desert such an oppressive institution. That might happily
solve quite a few of the world's problems since it would insure the church's
collapse. The church is literally sustained by the energy of women: women
volunteering their labor; women gratefully accepting minimum salaries for jobs
men are well-paid to do; women tithing from the money they themselves earn
or from the household budget; women running all the auxiliary functions of
the parish; women caring for and teaching children; women at the organ and
in the choir loft; women in the church kitchen, women preparing and feeding,
women washing dishes and cleaning, women serving-always-serving; women
most of all in the nuclear family, guaranteeing the stability of each unit of the
congregation and thus of the congregation itself and guaranteeing as well the
perpetuation of Christian (i.e., masculist) principles in the home. We are ourselves the enemy's strongest troops.

But the matter is not so simple. Though thousands are doing it, women,
even conscious women, find it hard to pick up and leave the church. We women
are incurable reformists and we believe the church needs us to help it reform.
We have to examine—all too briefly here—the following areas: (1) What happens
now to Lesbians/women/feminists who believe in reform? (2) What are the
dangers for feminists of remaining in the church? (3) What are the conceivable
reasons for remaining? and (4) What are the absolute pre-conditions for remaining?

(1) When we first begin to get in touch with our identity as women, when
we begin to haul away all the debris that has separated us from our self, we
seem suddenly also in touch with a tremendous energy bank. Out of that
energy we determine to educate the church that we love so much, to reform
it as we liberate ourselves. We gird our loins; we go forth into battle—usually
as a single soldier in quixotic attack upon the mighty fortress that represents
the patriarchy in our home town. We change the words of hymns, we insist on
"chairperson," we have ladies' Sundays, we create bible studies on the role of
women in the scriptures, we point out the sexism in church school literature,
we run for church councils and we may even enter seminary. We spend large
amounts of time convincing others and our self that things are improving. We

are exhilarated at our small victories; we despair at the more frequent defeats. The defeats come particularly hard when we realize that often the women—not the men—of the local church are most vehement against us.

The story is very old by now, and we know it well. If we are really making noises that cannot be ignored, and if the church really senses that we are dangerous, our rebelliousness may become a matter of concern. Our objections have somehow made us more attractive. ("I like a woman who gives me a little fight.") And so as individuals, we are separated out and awarded a crumb of power, for which we are expected to be undyingly grateful—an ordination, or a place on a "special commission," or the directive to start a task force, or a comparatively high-salaried job within the many-tiered structure. Whatever the crumb, our energy is now successfully channelled. We are adorned with garlands of red tape; we can be carefully watched. We can do less harm to the institution. We are *divided* (from our self, from our sisters) and *conquered* (subdued, quieted, co-opted, tokenized, shut-up) by the man, by the church structure, by the earthly emissary of the divine patriarch. How much do we dare to complain in the very household of the provider who gives us such dainty luxuries? And how can we hope to get together in feminist action with all our sisters when we our self have more power than they? More than once women in such positions in the church have expressed the feeling that they have been "had," that they have been "bought." The pattern smacks just a bit too much of a time-honored and debasing ritual that goes on between women and men.

We begin to see then that the Christian church and the feminism to which we're feeling daily more connected are fundamentally incompatible. We come to the awareness finally, that reformism will not do; that the church cannot be changed; that its identification depends upon a structure and a theology that are antithetical to the very existence of whole persons. We realize that no matter how hard we work to alter it, the church *to be the church* must continue its dehumanizing practices. It is the enemy of feminism and the enemy of woman. For the church to "become" what it must in order to be humanized (womanized, Lesbianized), it will first of all have to commit unequivocal suicide.

So now we erstwhile reformists wrestle with the real question: given our emotional/spiritual needs; our economic circumstance, if we are employed by the church; our new-found conviction that the church cannot be changed;

finally, our growing commitment to our self and to other women—given all this
—can we personally remain in the church? What do we lose, what do we gain,
if we leave?

When we finally have the courage to ask that question, it's not as if we're
deciding about changing jobs or moving to another city. The church is a part
of us. We have probably lived in it and it in us all of our lives. When we dare
to ask this question we are often right on the brink of terror and insanity, for
we are approaching a decision—we who are so ill-trained to decide—that seems
actually to split our brain, to tear our flesh. Even if we are fortunate enough
to be able to "taper off" with the church, to just stop going, to replace it with
other more fulfilling activities, still it rises to haunt us in the most subtle ways
and in the most unexpected circumstances, until we are ultimately forced to
deal with what living in the Christian church has meant to us.

The personal questions are a struggle. The strategic questions—those that
account for both the immediate and the long-run effect of our action on others,
on the whole society—can be an even deeper struggle. They demand that we
look at all women, at our own womanness/Lesbianism and at the efforts of
those who fight the same battle from another front.

(2) With this in mind, we have to ask: What are the dangers if we stay with
the church? First of all, will we be helping to inspire hope in the system? The
more Lesbians/women there are who gain voices in the church, for instance, or
the more Gay men there are who are ordained, the more inclined we are to
forget what it is that they and we are becoming a part of. Will we begin to
feel—and will thousands of others feel, too—that the church isn't so bad after
all? Will we forget that its structure and theology are dedicated to our self-
hatred and submission? Will we forget that we are not there to change it but
to dismantle it? Do we remember that we survive in it only because we must?

Second, how will we stay close to our self and to our sisters when we are
tempted with the benefits the church will offer us? When we become a token
woman on a board will we very prettily thank the powers that put us there or
will we insist that the board should be 60 percent women—or 100 percent
feminists if we're serious about wiping clean the slate of masculist thinking?
Will we be co-opted into the old mating games? Will we be seeking male
approval? Will we "talk nice" and be "feminine" so they'll hear us? *Will* they
hear us if we don't? Do we dare to find out? Will we our self, separated by
tokenism, become the enemy that feminists fight so hard against? If we are

THE MIRACLE OF LESBIANISM

participating in the oppressive structure is there anything that can keep us—in our heads and in our behavior—from becoming a part of the enemy?

Finally, if we stay, what happens to our energy? Is it being expended in the detailed and irrelevant operations that keep the bureaucracy going? Are we spending all of our self in argument with district directors or education commissions? Are they hearing us? *Can* they hear us? What in the meantime is happening to the women who really need our energy and whose energy we need? When they give us their support and we are fired up to go back and fight the hierarchy, are we not ripping off *their* energy too as we wade through one draining session after another with the established structures? What tangible benefits do our sisters get from our being there? Do they—do we—experience any of our real self?

(3) But there may be good reasons—not rationalizations—for remaining within the church even after we know we can't change it. There may be as many as four—each of them fraught with its own clear danger or unlikelihood. First, we may remain because the church is giving us employment. A job is a job within the system. If we need one, the church is as good an employer as any. If it pays more than we need, we can make sure that some money goes to help other women as well as our self. If we don't mind being split in two—that is, if we can separate our jobs from our creative lives—then we can put in a minimum of time and energy and draw our checks and save our real self for what's happening with women *outside* the church.

Second, we may remain in the church because women outside the church are only beginning to explore and affirm (or reaffirm) the "religious" parts of themselves. At least in the church our spiritual needs have some affirmation, if not some fulfillment.

Third, we may remain in a church job or even continue to volunteer within the church in order to learn some skills that will help us survive in a man's world. These skills will most assuredly be competitive ones. We can perhaps learn how to use them and how to share them for the protection and survival of other women as well as our self. Such skills might consist of simply learning how the system functions and where the money is and how to channel it into feminist purposes.

Fourth, we may remain as a church member and/or paid staff in order to make room for other women. It's not likely that we can help them get into monied jobs within the church, but we may be able to create some opportunities for women to get together and find themselves, their feminism. Then too over a slow and tortuous period of time, we may fill committee positions or jobs with feminists, play the games, make ourselves indispensable and then either take over or pull out and let whatever we were holding up collapse. It's hard to envision this happening on more than a local level. And, if we're going to engage in such Machiavellian tactics, we're going to have to be a lot tougher than experience suggests we can be without becoming totally alienated from our self.

(4) If we remain in the church we constantly have to reassess our circumstances to see to it that all of the minimum conditions for our survival there are intact. We need to do this without fail, like checking our oxygen supply on the moon. If any one of the conditions is lacking it must be remedied or we must leave.

First, within our self we must maintain our feminist consciousness, our commitment to our self, to other women and we must promote our constant growth in these things. We need to feel at a fundamental level that feminism is a lifetime commitment and is the minute-by-minute priority for that lifetime. We need to remember that we can't escape it because it's who we *are.* We need to be constantly aware that our life and our very being are neither Christian nor churchly. We are not there for institutional change but only to survive while we do our real movement work outside the walls of the church.

Second, we have to know that we are not alone. That does not just mean that we have a support group of women outside the church whom we can lean upon once a week. It means that there must exist a strong and committed group of feminists *within the church* with whom we are in daily contact. It means serious and regular strategy meetings with them and a clear sense on everyone's part that the group is *the* priority, the *sine qua non* for surviving as a feminist inside the structure. It means as well that we are *living* with—going home at night to—other women or perhaps rarely to men who are as committed to feminism as we are, committed to women's issues and to demonstrating that commitment by loud voices and consistent actions in the outside world, particularly in the church. Finally, it has to mean that we are in communication with whatever other groups there are within the church or within the community (such as Gay men, Third World and poor people) whose pain, along with our own, may be lessened if we can turn the church's resources toward them. Careful coalitions may be possible around issues of common concern.

Third, an absolute condition of our staying is our certain knowledge of our willingness to risk and to know when to risk. "Freedom's just another word for nothing left to lose," Janis Joplin sings. We need to be prepared every minute to say or do whatever outrageous thing is necessary with the full knowledge that we may well lose money, position, or prestige. We need to know with a clear and deep sense that anything we might "lose" we really didn't "have" to begin with. More important, we have to know—*really* know in a way that is connected to our guts, our history, our minds, and all the surrounding circumstances—that when we choose *not* to challenge the situation, then it is out of *wisdom* and not out of *fear* that we make that choice. We have to know that it is strategy that stops us and not a disconnected ego motive.

If we can handle the dangers, if we can find good reasons and if we have the necessary pre-conditions, we may be able to survive as feminists within the church. Every day leaving must be seen as an option; and every day the price of our staying and the price of our leaving must be calculated. The struggle continues, and it belongs to us all—to every individual woman from the moment she begins to question. And the rest of us must support her struggle however it turns out.

Feminists Leaving the Church

Often, in our religious lives the experience of doubt has in the end served to strengthen our faith. But there is a new challenge in these times which requires that Christians and most particularly Christian women see themselves at a critical point in their relationship to the church. The faith that Lesbians/women have lived and the devotion we have given to Father-Son-Holy Ghost and to our "fellow man" are being questioned by a source that seems as ancient and good as we have believed god himself to be. The source has no vocabulary with which to clarify and no syllogisms with which to justify. It has not been researched or documented or analyzed. The knowing of it is in the marrow of our bones, in the soles of our feet, in roots that reach below the rivers of our madness. Because it rises from inside us and carries with it the ordeals of our centuries of silence, it jars us in our daily Christian tasks and calls us to stand quiet so that we may hear.

What can this new source mean to us as Lesbians/women? Let us say it aloud and with courage. For many it has meant, and for many more it will mean that we who have called ourselves Christians have been duped by an increasingly rigid, intensely motivated, and deeply complex historical process. The "blame" cannot be placed upon any individual, since the secret of the

system's wide success lies in the fact that it is an anonymous institutionaliza-
tion of an attitude.

We resist the idea of "some other god but Yaweh" or the suggestion that
the Jesus of history was deliberately mystified into the Christ of faith. We resist in part because we do not want to admit our gullibility. Such an admission is particularly hard for those of us who have just begun to deny the
"stupid" image that has been our inheritance under the patriarchy. But integrity demands that we admit just that. We have been teased, cajoled, flattered,
humiliated and even threatened—not to say actually physically coerced—into
believing in the eternal, external and exclusive existence of the great father-
god, and in the man-made theological fabrications that surround his name.
In serving the external god, we have neglected a dormant part of ourselves
which we know in our depths to be real and honest: the woman-god, however
she is named, who speaks not from outside but from within us, from the
ground of our own experience as individuals and from the flow that moves
among women. That ground and that flow combine into our touchstone of
truth, even in the face of thousands of years of testicular theology and abstract propaganda.

It is not true. What all of our lives have meant, it is not true. We stand at
this crossroads in our personal history and know what we must know, feel
what we must feel, relinquish what we must relinquish. It is not true. Whatever rationalizations we muster, however much we hope for the church's re-
newal, however warm and deep our memories are of "fellowship" and love,
liturgy and song, we are brought to truth with the knowledge that none of it
has ever sustained us—except at the price of our own strength and our own
freedom. In the face of the call to identify ourselves, in the face of the pain
that we can now embrace, in the face of our impending self-love and the sharing of our new-found gospel-selves with other women—in the face of all that,
we cannot look upward again to the towering father-god or accept his death-
dealing commandments. His thundering voice becomes a petulant whine; but we
are too full of our own insurgent life to nurture him any longer.

Many of us must go. We leave behind in the church others whom we love
and who love us but who, for reasons they alone must state, will not join us.
We leave them with a knowledge that they have in themselves, if they will but
listen and hear: that the Christian church is a great and splendid drama, but it
plays the boards in the service of falsehood and woman-hatred. We move out
and away from it with sorrow—but with the certain knowledge that something

new is happening with women in this century: the pain of a new birth, a new life, that means a redemptive change in the course of human history.

CONCLUSION

It must be clear by now that women and the Gay movement are not begging the church for simple justice within the system. We do not even insist that it is incumbent upon the church to confess, repent, apologize and make redress of the world's grievances against it. Feminists, Lesbians and Gay men are not merely indicting the church for its embarrassingly contradictory attitudes toward women and Gay persons. Feminism, Lesbians and Gay liberation (insofar as it stands on a feminist base), challenge the very existence of the woman-hating hierarchical and exclusively masculist Judeo-Christian tradition. We maintain that the gospel message calling for love of our whole self as well as of others does not and cannot live within the Christian church.

Women, Gay people, national liberation struggles, the poor and even nature herself are all giving clear and unmistakable signals that the church must go, that the rule of the patriarchal mind-set must end.

If it continues, then we will not survive. If we allow it to continue, we do not deserve to survive.

NOTES

1. *Inge K. Broverman, et al., "Sex-Role Stereotypes and Clinical Judgments of Mental Health,"* Journal of Consulting and Clinical Psychology, *vol. 34, no. 1 (1970). Available from Inge K. Broverman, Worcester State Hospital, Worcester, Massachusetts 01604.*

2. *Del Martin and Phyllis Lyon,* Lesbian/Woman *(San Francisco: Glide Publications, 1972), p. 84. See also the mid-1950s survey by Daughters of Bilitis, 1005 Market, No. 208, San Francisco, California, 94103.*

3. *Janis Kelly, "Sister Love: An Exploration of the Need for Homosexual Experience,"* Non-Traditional Family Forms in the 1970's, *published by the National Council on Family Relations, 1219 University Avenue Southeast, Minneapolis, Minnesota 55414 (1972).*

4. *As documented in* Women and the Word, *available through the Office of Women's Affairs, Graduate Theological Union, 2465 LeConte, Berkeley,*

California 94707. The direct references are: A. Richardson, ed., A Theological Word Book of the Bible *(New York: Macmillan, 1951), pp. 94, 97;* The Oxford Universal Dictionary, *third edition; S. L. MacGregor Mathers, trans.*, Hebrew Literature, The Kabbala Unveiled *(London: George Redway, 1901), pp. iv-v, 318, 337, 359-60;* The Interpreter's Dictionary of the Bible *(New York: Abingdon Press, 1962), vol. A-D, pp. 42-43; vol. K-Q, p. 243; vol. R-Z, p. 300.*

SELECTED BIBLIOGRAPHY

GAY PEOPLE

Lesbians

Abbott, Sidney, and Barbara Love. *Sappho Was a Right-On Woman.* New York: Stein and Day, 1972. Also in paper.
An exploration of Lesbian life-styles and politics by two open Lesbians. Particularly fine in its examination of Lesbianism's historical connections to the women's movement.

Brown, Rita Mae. *Ruby Fruit Jungle.* Plainfield, Vermont: Daughters, Inc., 1973.
A novel lifted up from the pain and the laughter of a working class Lesbian's life experience. Rich reading in one of the important perspectives on Lesbianism.

Johnston, Jill. *Lesbian Nation: The Feminist Solution.* New York: Simon and Schuster, 1973.
Much stream-of-consciousness writing. Lesbian feminists will particularly enjoy the recreation of the past and the projection of a vision.

Martin, Del,and Phyllis Lyon. *Lesbian/Woman.* San Francisco: Glide Publications, 1972. Also in paper from Bantam.
Probably the best book for beginning to understand Lesbianism. Highly personalized and anecdotal history and exploration of life-styles and oppression. By two open Lesbians.

Miller, Isabel. *Patience and Sarah.* New York: McGraw-Hill, 1969.
An historical novel about two nineteenth-century women who love each other. The warm story of their struggles to be together.

Rosen, David H. *Lesbianism: A Study of Female Homosexuality.* Springfield, Illinois: Charles C. Thomas, 1973.
Many conscious Lesbians will explode to see still another study of Lesbianism by a straight male doctor. But this book is valuable because it reviews and takes to task psychiatric literature on the subject, indicting that literature as sexist, morally biased, and scientifically inaccurate.

Wolff, Charlotte. *Love between Women.* New York: St. Martin's Press, 1971.
A questionable source since it seems at points to be only warmed-over Freud. Important, however, because the author, an M.D., does seem to feel that Lesbians are the original liberated women.

Gay Men

Altman, Dennis. *Homosexual: Oppression and Liberation.* New York: Outerbridge and Dienstfrey (through Dutton), 1971.
This book reflects an unusual awareness of feminism. The author limits himself to the male homosexual. A solid study of the comparisons and contrasts of the Gay movement and other movements.

Churchill, Wainwright. *Homosexual Behavior among Males: A Cross-cultural and Cross-species Investigation.* New York: Hawthorn Books, 1967.
The presentation by a neuro-psychiatrist of truths about same-sex relationships. Churchill begins with an exploration of the responsibility of the Judeo-Christian tradition for the "sin and sickness" mentality.

Clarke, Lige,and Jack Nichols. *I Have More Fun with You Than Anybody.* New York: St. Martin's Press, 1972.
The story of two Gay men's multi-dimensional loving relationship. A myth-smasher.

Fisher, Peter. *The Gay Mystique: The Myth and Reality of Male Homosexuality.* New York: Stein and Day, 1972.
The best book to date concerning Gay men. Very helpful to heterosexual people in understanding the Gay man's reality. Puts to rest the myths surrounding Gay relationships and Gay people in professions.

Perry, Troy. *The Lord Is My Shepherd and He Knows I'm Gay.* Los Angeles: Nash Publishing Co., 1972.
An autobiographical account of the changes in the life of the founder of the Metropolitan Community Church—his struggles as a Christian, a father, a minister, and a Gay man.

Richmond, Len,and Gary Noguera. *The Gay Liberation Book.* San Francisco: Ramparts, 1973.
Some well-known men join in this commentary upon the Gay liberation movement, 1969-1971. Poetry, drawings, pictures make this book comfortable to read.

Weinberg, George. *Society and the Healthy Homosexual.* New York: St. Martin's Press, 1972.
A clinical psychologist discusses society's homophobia and the bias of psychiatry against same-sex relationships. Internal reality of Gay person is related to familial and cultural patterns. Contains good information on communication with parents.

Gay Liberation

Freedman, Mark. *Homosexuality and Psychological Functioning.* Belmont, Calif.: Wadsworth Publishing Co., 1971.
In its language and concepts more for the professional than for the layperson. Often quoted for its documentation of the Lesbian's comparatively greater self-actualization among American women.

Jay, Karla,and Allen Young, eds. *Out of the Closets: Voices of Gay Liberation.* New York: Douglas/Links Books, 1972.
A collection of some of the Gay movement's best essays from the underground press. The more radical view.

Lee, Ronald. "Gay Liberation and Mental Health." *The National Conference on Social Welfare,* Proceedings, 1972. New York: Columbia University Press, 1972. The mental-health profession heard an openly Gay man, one of its own highly credentialed professionals, call for change. A paper read at this conference.

Martin, Del, and Paul Mariah. "Homosexual Love—Woman to Woman, Man to Man." *Love Today: A New Exploration.* Herbert A. Otto, ed. New York: Association Press, 1972.
A Lesbian and a Gay man explore the reality of same-sex relationships, tracing the nature and effect of societal attitudes toward such relationships. A good introduction to the subject.

Oberholtzer, W. Dwight, ed. *Is Gay Good? Ethics, Theology, and Homosexuality.* Philadelphia: The Westminister Press, 1971.
Writings in response to an article from the early sixties called "Toward a Theology of Homosexuality." One article on the Lesbian approach; otherwise mostly on men. Offensive to many Gay people because of its liberalism.

Tobin, Kay, and Randy Wicker. *The Gay Crusaders.* New York: Paperback Library, 1972.
Personal stories of Gay women and men who were among the first openly to challenge society's oppressiveness. A really authentic flavor comes across from the collection of interviews.

Wetge, Ralph W., ed. *The Same Sex: An Appraisal of Homosexuality.* Philadelphia: Pilgrim Press, 1969.
Probably the first professional book that brought in Gay writers as authorities on the subject of Gayness. Barbara Gittings, Frank Kameny and Foster Gunnison concentrate on the relationship of the homosexual (largely male) to the law, to ethics, and to society.

Human Sexuality

Barnett, Walter. *Sexual Freedom and the Constitution, An Inquiry into the Constitutionality of Repressive Sex Laws.* Albuquerque: University of New Mexico Press, 1973.
A law professor analyzes sex laws, among them proscriptions against certain sex acts between consenting adults which affect heterosexual and homosexual people alike.

Brecher, Ruth, and Edward Brecher. *An Analysis of Human Sexual Response.* New York: New American Library, 1966. Signet paper.
A layperson's reader in the sexuality research of Virginia Johnson and W. H. Masters. The experiments of these doctors along with the Kinsey studies have de-mythified and de-mystified human sexuality.

Kinsey, A. C., W. B. Pomeroy and C. E. Martin. *Sexual Behavior in the Human Male* and *Sexual Behavior in the Human Female.* Philadelphia: Saunders, 1948 and 1953 respectively.
The research that helped to turn Americans toward a re-evaluation of sexuality and of morality. Often very technical.

Otto, Herbert A., ed. *The New Sexuality.* Palo Alto, Calif.: Science and Behavior Books, Inc., 1971.
Anthologized with articles on group marriage, nudity, premarital sex and the like, Del Martin and Phyllis Lyon's article on homosexuality deals with Gay relationships, Gay marriages, and the Judeo-Christian influence on attitudes toward Gay people.

Seaman, Barbara. *Free and Female: The Sex Life of the Contemporary Woman.* New York: Coward, McCann and Geoghegan, Inc., 1972.
Though male-identified, the author seems to move toward feminism. She deals far too briefly with Lesbianism and homosexuality, but her few remarks are right-on.

Sherfey, Mary Jane. *The Nature and Evolution of Female Sexuality.* New York: Random House, 1972.
A development of the thesis that the reason men have held women down is their fear of the female's tremendous sensual and sexual superiority. Some feminists are disappointed in the author's male-identification.

THE WOMEN'S MOVEMENT

From and Toward Feminism

Bengis, Ingrid. *Combat in the Erogenous Zone, Writings on Love, Hate, and Sex.* New York: Alfred A. Knopf, 1972. Also in paper.
An internal odyssey that moves through feelings about three areas: man-hating, Lesbianism, and love. Both Lesbians and heterosexual women find self-affirmation in this book.

Bird, Carolyn. *Born Female: The High Cost of Keeping Women Down.* New York: Pocket Books, 1970. Paper.
Factual account of women's economic situation. Good reading for those just getting in touch with women's place.

Cade, Toni, ed. *The Black Woman.* New York: New American Library, 1970. Signet paper.
Excellent collection of writings by Black women exploring a wide range of topics. A book that will change the ordinary white reader's outlook.

Chesler, Phyllis. *Women and Madness.* New York: Doubleday, 1972. Also in paper.
An indictment of the psychiatric profession's deliberate and unconscious contributions to women's madness. The woman reader experiences "yeah-yeah! " feelings.

Cooke, Joanne, Charlotte Bunch-Weeks, and Robin Morgan, eds. *The New Woman.* Greenwich, Connecticut: Fawcett Publications, 1971. Paper.
A re-publication of the March-April 1969 issue of *Motive* magazine (published by the United Methodist Church). It caused a furor among church people because of its audacity and among women because of its truth-speaking.

Davis, Elizabeth Gould. *The First Sex.* New York: G. P. Putnam's Sons, 1971. Also in Penguin paper.
Astonishing historical data about ancient matriarchies and woman's place in the patriarchy. The speculation sometimes soars above the evidence, but then, so does the positive self-image of the woman reader.

de Beauvoir, Simone. *The Second Sex.* New York: Alfred A. Knopf, 1952. Also in Bantam paper.
A deep analysis of woman's nature—biological, psychological, social—and an exploration of her history. By now a classic in the movement, it is heavy stimulating reading.

Diner, Helen. *Mothers and Amazons, The First Feminine History of Culture.* New York: Julian Press, 1965. Also in Anchor paper.
An important attempt to look at the history that came before the patriarchy. Lots of astonishing documented material and some well-justified speculation upon it.

Firestone, Shulamith. *The Dialectic of Sex, The Case for Feminist Revolution.* New York: William Morrow and Co., 1970. Also in paper.
Essential reading for feminists. Excellent analysis of who women have been, where they are now and how they should use the advances of society. Lots to agree with, lots to disagree with. A thin analysis of relationship to race and class.

Gould, Lois. "Stories for Free Children: X—A Fabulous Child's Story." *Ms.,* vol. 1, no. 6 (December 1972), 74.
Struggles of parents and their child of unnamed sex against a society that has to have sex-roles to relate to. (*Ms.* magazine is $9.00 per year from 123 Garden Street, Marion, Ohio.)

Greer, Germaine. *The Female Eunuch.* London: Paladin Press, 1971. Also in paper.
Some thought it outrageous, others mild. An analysis of love and sex in a man's world in contrast to the author's own ideas and feelings about personal relationships.

Lerner, Gerder. *Black Women in White America.* New York: Vintage, 1972.
Writings of Black women about their lives. A documentary from mid-nineteenth century to the present on the conditions molding Black people.

Marine, Gene. *A Male Guide to Women's Liberation.* New York: Holt, Rinehart and Winston, 1972.
As yet the best attempt to clarify the meaning of women's liberation to men. Written by a man for men.

Mellaart, James. *Catul Hüyük, A Neolithic Town in Anatolia.* New York: McGraw-Hill, 1967.
Highly scholarly presentation by a well-known archaeologist of architecture, sculpture, paintings, and crafts from an ancient city and an assessment of the matriarchal society they represent.

Millett, Kate. *Sexual Politics.* Garden City, New York: Doubleday, 1970. Also in paper.
Scholarly literary criticism that speaks in a loud voice about sexual relations as the model for power relationships. Exciting, if heavy, reading.

Montagu, Ashley. *The Natural Superiority of Women.* New York: Macmillan, 1957.
A highly respected anthropologist lays out the case for female superiority. He examines genetics, biology, psychology, sociology. This book, one of the first on the subject, has recently been resurrected.

Morgan, Robin, ed. *Sisterhood Is Powerful.* New York: Random House, 1970. Also in paper.
Probably still the best starting place for reading about women's growing consciousness. A varied and extensive anthology of feminist writings.

Roszak, Betty, and Theodore Roszak. *Masculine/Feminine, Readings in Sexual Mythology and the Liberation of Women.* New York: Harper and Row, 1969. Paper.
Collection of feminist (and misogynist) writings, mainly from the nineteenth and twentieth centuries. An excellent starting point for understanding feminism.

Women and the Church

Daly, Mary. *The Church and the Second Sex.* New York: Harper and Row, 1968.
A theological examination of the Christian church's sexism. It is as if the author is in this book clearing her throat before delivering her message in *Beyond God the Father.*

Daly, Mary. *Beyond God the Father.* Boston: Beacon Press, 1973.
An assessment of sexist theology and a recommendation for the exorcism of internalized role stereotypes. A strong statement. A vision.

Doely, Sarah Bentley, ed. *Women's Liberation and the Church.* New York: Association Press, 1970.
An early and important anthology of eight women's assessment of woman's place within the Christian tradition. Some anger, some conciliation.

Graves, Robert, and Raphael Patai. *Hebrew Myths, The Book of Genesis.* London: Cassell and Company, Ltd., 1963.
Explication in a righteously documented manner of variations on well-known Genesis stories. A background for understanding many of the contradictions in the scriptures. Particularly important to the beginnings of feminist archaeology and research.

Hewitt, Emily, and Suzanne Hiatt. *Women Priests: Yes or No.* New York: Seabury, 1973. Paper.
Although the Episcopal hierarchy to which this book is probably addressed is deaf to its voice, the work is a skilled and persuasive argument effectively countering all the objections to the ordination of women.

Keen, Sam. *To a Dancing God.* New York: Harper and Row, 1970. Paper.
Keen is one of the few men to suggest a new and (though he does not specify it as such) womanly starting place for the knowing of God. A proposal for a visceral theology.

McGrath, Sister Albertus Magnus. *What a Modern Catholic Believes about Women.* Chicago: Thomas More, 1972. Paper.
A documentation of the Roman Catholic Church's attitude toward women. Reaches back into early church and into scriptures to examine views on the subject.

Morris, Joan. *The Lady Was a Bishop.* New York: Macmillan, 1973.
The author wanted to title this book "The Hidden History of Women in the Church." She builds the case yet again against the church's practice of making women invisible.

Reik, Theodor. *The Creation of Woman.* New York: McGraw-Hill, 1960. Paper.
"A psychoanalytic inquiry into the myth of Eve." A challenge to western misogyny from an unusual source. Well documented. Easy reading.

Ruether, Rosemary Radford. *The Radical Kingdom: The Western Experience of Messianic Hope.* New York: Harper and Row, 1970.
Lucid presentation and analysis of rebellious thinking within the Christian tradition, much of it in line with feminist thinking. Only occasional direct reference to women's actual or potential contributions.

Ruether, Rosemary Radford. *Liberation Theology: Human Hope Confronts Christian History and American Power.* New York: Paulist Press, 1972.
This book explores with the author's characteristic intellectual integrity the common sources of oppression and seeks to encourage potential understanding among liberation movements rather than their opposition to each other.

SELECTED ARTICLES ON HOMOSEXUALITY IN RELIGIOUS PERIODICALS

Baum, Gregory. "Catholic Homosexuals." *Commonweal.* February 15, 1974.

DePuy, Norman. "God's Gays."* *American Baptist.* October 1971. Reprints from the Minnesota Council for the Church and the Homophile, 122 West Franklin Ave., Minneapolis, Minnesota, 55404.

*Reprinted in *Connexion*, May 1973. Available from United Ministries in Higher Education, Room 708, 3 W. 29, New York, New York, 10001, 25¢.

Driver, Tom F. "The Contemporary and Christian Contexts." *Commonweal.*
April 6, 1973.

Fehren, Father Henry. "A Christian Response to Homosexuals." *U. S. Catholic.*
September, 1972.

Fink, Peter E. "A Pastoral Hypothesis." *Commonweal.* April 6, 1973.

Gearhart, Sally. "The Lesbian and God-the-Father, or, All the Church Needs Is
a Good Lay—on Its Side."* *Radical Religion: Feminism and Religion,* vol. I,
no. 2, Spring 1974. 2323 Hearst St., Berkeley, California, 94709. Also available from *Genesis III,* P. O. Box 24003, Philadelphia, Pennsylvania, 19139
for 15¢ in stamps or coin plus stamped self-addressed No. 10 envelope; 15
copies for $2.00 postpaid.

"Homosexuality: Neither Sin nor Sickness." The July-August, 1973 issue of
Trends. Available for $1.00 per copy from *Trends,* Room 200, Witherspoon
Building, Philadelphia, Pennsylvania, 19107. Publication of the United Pres-
byterian Church.

Lerrigo, Charles. "MCC: The Church Comes Out." *New World Outlook.* New
Series, vol. 33, no. 9, May 1973. *New World Outlook,* 475 Riverside Drive,
New York, New York, 10027; 35¢ single copy, $3.00/dozen.

Lyon, Phyllis, and Tom Maurer. "Homosexuals Are Persons." *Spectrum.* Novem-
ber/December, 1971. Reprints from Council on Religion and the Homosexual,
83 McAllister, San Francisco, California, 94102.

McNeill, John. "The Homosexual and the Church." *National Catholic Reporter.*
Vol. 9, no. 38, October 5, 1973. Available from *National Catholic Reporter,*
115 E. Armour Blvd., Kansas City, Missouri, 64111. Single copies free.

Motive: Gay Men's Liberation Issue and *Lesbian/Feminist* Issue, each at $1.00.
Available from G. P. O. Box 1677, New York, New York, 10001. Last issues
of the United Methodist Church's publication, *Motive.*

Preston, John. "Gay, Proud, and Christian."* *Event.* Vol. 11, no. 3. March 1971.
Reprints from the Minnesota Council for the Church and the Homophile, 122
West Franklin Ave., Minneapolis, Minnesota, 55404.

Rash, John. "Reforming Pastoral Attitudes Towards Homosexuality." *The Union
Seminary Quarterly Review.* Vol. XXV, no. 4, Summer, 1970.

"To Accept Homosexuals." Editorial in *Christian Century.* March 3, 1971.

Trible, Phyllis. "Depatriarchalizing in Biblical Interpretation." *Journal of the
American Academy of Religion.* Vol. XLI, no. 1, March 1973.

Wright, Elliott. "The Church and Gay Liberation." *The Christian Century.*
March 3, 1971.

*Reprinted in *Connexion,* May 1973. Available from United Ministries in higher
Education, Room 708, 3 W. 29, New York, New York, 10001, 25¢.

RESOURCES

GAY / CHRISTIAN PERIODICALS

Dignity Newsletter. Bob Fournier, editor. 1624 Serrano, Los Angeles, California, 90027.

The Gay Christian, Journal of the Metropolitan Community Church of New York City. Bimonthly. 25¢ per copy, $5.00 per year. MCC/New York, G. P. O. Box 1757, New York, New York, 10001.

In Unity, Quarterly Magazine of the Universal Fellowship of Metropolitan Community Churches. $6.50 per year. G. P. O. Box 1757, New York, New York, 10001.

FILMS (ON SPECIAL ORDER)

"Holding," 16 mm color film, 15 minutes. Sexually graphic film dealing in a sensitive manner with several levels of a Lesbian relationship.
Sale: $200.00
Rental: $ 30.00
Multi-Media Resource Center, 540 Powell, San Francisco, California, 94108.

"Home Movie," 16 mm film, color and b/w, sound, 11 minutes. A Lesbian moves from the home movies showing her high school days to her present Lesbian life-style. A self-affirming, woman-affirming film.
Sale: $100.00
Rental: $ 20.00
Multi-Media Resource Center, 540 Powell, San Francisco, California, 94108.

"The Invisible Minority: The Homosexuals in our Society," filmstrip, sound, color, 60 minutes.
Sale only: $60.00
Produced by and available from the Unitarian Universalist Association, 25 Beacon Street, Boston, Massachusetts, 02108.

"Lavender," 16 mm color film, 13 minutes. A sensitive, honest portrait of a Lesbian couple.
Sale: $170.00
Rental: $ 17.00
Perennial Education, Inc., 1825 Willow Road, P. O. Box 236, Northfield, Illinois, 60093.

"A Position of Faith," 16 mm, color, 18 minutes. Explores the controversial issues surrounding the ordination of Bill Johnson to the ministry of the United Church of Christ.
Sale: $250.00
Rental: $ 25.00
McGraw-Hill/Contemporary Films, 330 W. 42, New York, New York, 10036.

"Sandy and Madeleine's Family," 16 mm, color, 29 minutes. Documents the struggle of Lesbian mothers, Sandra Schuster and Madeleine Isaacson, to win custody of their six children.
Sale: $200.00
Rental: $ 40.00
Multi-Media Resource Center, 540 Powell, San Francisco, California, 94108.

"Vir Amat," 16 mm, color, 15 minutes. Sexually graphic film that de-mythologizes the impersonality (so-called) of Gay male relationships by sharing the sexual pattern of a young male couple.
Sale: $200.00
Rental: $ 30.00
Multi-Media Resource Center, 540 Powell, San Francisco, California, 94108.

ARTICLES, PACKETS, BOOKS, PAMPHLETS, AND DIRECTORIES (ON SPECIAL ORDER)

Asian Women. An important anthology of Asian women's understandings of themselves, particularly against the background of the U. S. social scene. Available from Asian Women, 3405 Dwinelle Hall, University of California, Berkeley, California, 94720. $2.00.

Blamires, David. *Homosexuality from the Inside.* 1973. A sober and informed account of the position and feelings of a group of Gay Quakers. A brief (42 pages) introduction to the topic from a Gay perspective. Order from Friends Book Store, 302 Arch St., Philadelphia, Pennsylvania, 19106, 95¢ plus 30¢ postage handling for single copy, 50¢ handling for 2 or more.

Churchmen Speak Out for Homosexual Law Reform. A compendium of statements by religious leaders. Available from Council on Religion and the Homosexual, 83 McAllister, San Francisco, California, 94102. $1.00.

Gay Bibliography. 1974. A source of up-to-date information on Gay publications. The task force that puts it out is the first group of openly Gay people to come together within a profession. Probably the best ongoing source available. Order free bibliographies (donations welcome) from the Task Force on Gay Liberation of the Social Responsibilities Round Table of the American Library Association, c/o Barbara Gittings, P. O. Box 2383, Philadelphia, Pennsylvania, 19103.

Gayellow Pages. Classified directory of Gay businesses, services, and organizations. Box 292, Village Station, New York, New York, 10014. $5.00.

Hope, Glenda, Rev. Ms. *Women People—Gay People—Church People.* Address by a heterosexual feminist delivered to the annual meeting (1974) of the Council on Religion and the Homosexual. Order from CRH, 83 McAllister, San Francisco, California, 94102. 25¢.

International List of Gay Organizations. Gay Activists Alliance, Box 2, Village Station, New York, New York, 10014. $1.00.

Learning from Experience: The Ordination of an Affirmed Homosexual Person. Struggles of heterosexual people in coming to understand Gay people and the church. Available from Northern California Conference of the United Church of Christ, Room 677, Flood Building, 870 Market Street, San Francisco, California, 94102. $2.00 per copy and at bulk rates.

Lee, Ronald, *et al. Gay Men Speak.* 1973. In "The Yes Book of Sex" series. Available from Multi-Media Resource Center, 540 Powell, San Francisco, California, 94108. $1.95.

Lesbians Speak Out. A 1970 collection of essays by Lesbians and probably the first of its kind. New edition from The Women's Press Collective, 5251 Broadway, Oakland, California, 94618. $2.00.

Martin, Del, and Phyllis Lyon. *Lesbian Love and Liberation.* 1973. In "The Yes Book of Sex" series. Available from Multi-Media Resource Center, 540 Powell, San Francisco, California, 94108. $1.95.

Mitchell, Bernice. "Secrets of Genesis," in *Women Out of History.* 1972. Feminist examination of creation narratives. Available from Ann Forfreedom, editor, Peace Press, 3828 Willat Ave., Culver City, California, 90230. $3.00.

Moreno, Dorinda, ed. *La Mujer en Pie de Lucha.* Chicana women speak in both Spanish and English of themselves, their heritage, and their circumstances. Available from La Raza Studies, San Francisco State University, 69 Campus Circle, San Francisco, California, 94132. $8.00.

N. O. W. Resolutions in support of Lesbianism and Lesbian mothers' rights. Available from the National Organization for Women, National Office, 5 South Wabash, Suite 1615, Chicago, Illinois, 60603. Passed in 1971 and 1973.

On Being Gay. 1973. Cassette tape. 60 minutes. A companion tape for the *Trends* issue on homosexuality but may be used alone as study guide. Questions for discussion, and interviews with adult and teenage Gay people, a doctor, a lawyer, a parish minister and a seminary president. Available from Thesis Creative Educational Resources, Box 11724, Pittsburgh, Pennsylvania, 15228. $5.98.

Report of the Committee on Homosexual Offences and Prostitution (The Wolfenden Report). 1957. The historic document that was the prelude to Great Britain's decriminalization of homosexuality. Available from Pendragon House, Inc., 899 Broadway Avenue, Redwood City, California, 94063. $2.30. Also in book form from Lancer Books.

Student Gay Groups. List of Gay groups at member colleges of National Student Association. Available from National Gay Student Center, 2115 S Street, N.W., Washington, D.C. 20008. 25¢.

The Woman Packet and *Women Exploring Theology.* The first on the position of women in church and society, the second a compilation of material from the 1972 and 1973 conferences in Grailville, Ohio. Available from Church Women United, Box 134, Mahattanville Station, New York, New York, 10027. $2.00 each.

The Woman's Bible is a commentary by nineteenth century feminists upon portions of the Bible dealing directly with women—or failing to do so. Available for $16.00 (for two volumes in one) from Arno Press, 330 Madison Avenue, New York, New York, 10017. Announcement of a forthcoming paper edition will be in *Genesis III,* P. O. Box 24003, Philadelphia, Pennsylvania, 19139.

Women. Probably the best collection of articles by women from Africa, Asia, Europe, the Middle East, Latin America, and North America. Available from the Women's Caucus of the United Ministries in Higher Education, P. O. Box 187, Dayton View Station, Dayton, Ohio, 45406. $1.50.

Women and the Word: Toward a Whole Theology. Women seminarians explore new perspectives on themselves and the theological process. Includes lectures by Peggy Way, Rosemary Ruether, and Nelle Morton. Available from Office of Women's Affairs, 2465 LeConte, Berkeley, California, 94709. $1.25 donation.

ORGANIZATIONS

Council on Religion and the Homosexual, Inc. (CRH).
83 McAllister Street, Suite 421, San Francisco, California, 94102,
(415) 863-2295.
CRH offers a variety of publications, speakers, and referrals. Maintains an up-to-date contact list of organizing efforts by Gay people in various denominations and in seminary communities. Presents an annual symposium.

Daughters of Bilitis (DOB)—a Lesbian organization.
1005 Market Street, No. 208, San Francisco, California, 94103, (415) 861-8689.
For DOB offices in other cities, contact DOB/San Francisco.

Denominational Gay Caucuses (contact CRH/San Francisco for more detailed information):
American Baptist Church
American Lutheran Church
Disciples of Christ
Episcopal Church
Lutheran Church in America
Missouri Synod Lutheran Church
Presbyterian Church in the U.S.
Reformed Church in America
Religious Society of Friends
Unitarian Universalist Association
United Church of Christ
United Methodist Church
United Presbyterian Church in the U. S. A.

Dignity/National Office
755 Boylston Street, Suite 514, Boston, Massachusetts, 02116

Lesbian Resource Center
710 West 22nd Street, Minneapolis, Minnesota, 55405.
Keeps up-to-date information on Lesbian activities across the nation.

Lincoln-Omaha Council on Religion and the Homosexual
Box 2323, Station B, Lincoln, Nebraska, 68502.

Milwaukee Council on Religion and the Homosexual
P. O. Box 90530, Milwaukee, Wisconsin, 53202

Minnesota Council for the Church and the Homophile
122 West Franklin Avenue, Minneapolis, Minnesota, 55404

Universal Fellowship of Metropolitan Community Churches
National Headquarters
373 North Western Avenue, Suite 211
Los Angeles, California, 90004